SUZE ORMAN'S
PROTECTION PORTFOLIO™

The Forms You Need Today to Protect Your Tomorrows

This product provides information and general advice about the law. But laws and procedures change frequently, and they can be interpreted differently by different people. For specific advice geared to your specific situation, consult an expert. No book, software, or other published material is a substitute for personalized advice from a knowledgeable lawyer licensed to practice law in your state.

Hay House, Inc.
Carlsbad, California • Sydney, Australia
Canada • Hong Kong • United Kingdom

Published and distributed in the United States by Hay House, Inc., P.O. Box 5100, Carlsbad, CA 92018-5100
(800) 654-5126 • (800) 650-5115 (fax) • www.hayhouse.com

ISBN 1-4019-0118-2

06 05 04 03   6 5 4 3
1st printing, June 2002
3rd printing, April 2003

Printed in the United States of America

DEAR FRIENDS,

I'm thrilled that you've taken the important step of protecting yourself and your loved ones by purchasing the Suze Orman Protection Portfolio™. The Protection Portfolio is unlike any other product, because it actually includes the forms and instructions to create and personalize your own advanced directive and durable power of attorney for health care, financial power of attorney, will, and revocable trust as well as many other essential forms and documents. Compiling these documents ahead of time will help prevent you and your family from going through the worry and confusion that can result when the unexpected occurs to a loved one and those who are left behind don't know how to locate vital legal and financial documents.

Obviously, since all of your situations are unique, you should always take these completed documents to your own lawyer to make sure they fit your needs. But having a lawyer look over completed documents versus doing it from scratch with him or her can be a serious cost-saving tool.

To help you protect your future and the futures of those you love, I've provided the following:

- **The CD-ROM, entitled "The Forms You Need to Protect Your Tomorrows."** This CD-ROM, compatible with both PC and Macintosh computers, includes essential forms that allow you to correct your credit report; request military records, Social Security annual statements, and copies of essential personal documents such as birth and marriage certificates; and even create a cohabitation agreement if you're living with someone. You'll also find a host of links to government and other Websites that will provide you with additional important forms to download.

- **Two instructional audio CDs, called "What You Need to Know Today to Protect Your Tomorrows."** Narrated by my personal trust attorney, Janet Dobrovolny, and myself, these CDs will take you step-by-step through the most important clauses in the four most critical documents on your CD-ROM: a will, a revocable living trust, an advanced directive and durable power of attorney for health care, and a financial power of attorney.

- **The Protection Portfolio guidebook, "The Forms You Need Today to Protect Your Tomorrows."** This guidebook includes many sample forms, and provides worksheets to help you make important financial calculations, checklists to ensure that you're thoroughly prepared for the what-if's of life, and detailed instructions and explanations about actions you must take to protect yourself and your loved ones—everything that you value.

- **The Protection Portfolio emergency contact cards.** These are cards on which to list your emergency names and numbers so that your loved ones always know whom to contact.

- **The Protection Portfolio password.** This password allows you to access the "protectionhelp" section of my Website, **www.suzeorman.com**, where you'll be able to obtain help if you're having trouble accessing your CD-ROM, completing a form or understanding any part of the Protection Portfolio system; and/or download new forms when changes in the law require a modification to the documents that are on your CD-ROM. This site will be maintained for as long as **www.suzeorman.com** is on-line.

To access "protectionhelp," please log on to **www.suzeorman.com** and click on the **protectionhelp** icon. You will be asked for a user name and password. Enter the following codes:
User Name: **asksuze**   Password: **rajas**

I sincerely hope that you enjoy your Protection Portfolio, and I thank you for your continued support.

All my love and respect,

[signature]

Note: Please see the next page for detailed instructions on how to load the CD-ROM onto your computer.

HOW TO OPEN THE FORMS CD-ROM ON YOUR COMPUTER

Insert the Protection Portfolio Forms CD-ROM into your computer's CD drive. It should automatically open in your browser. If your CD-ROM does not automatically open, please follow the directions below:

1. Open up your Internet browser (best viewed with the latest version of Internet Explorer).

2. Click on the "File" menu, and then click on "Open." A separate window will appear that will say "Open." Click on the "Browse" button.

3. Another window will open that says "Look in." Adjacent to the "Look in" box, click on the arrow pointing down.

4. Click on the drive where the PROTECT CD-ROM is located, probably the D drive.

5. Several file names will appear in the window. Double click on the file named "index" or "index.htm," and this will open the CD-ROM.

INTERNET EXPLORER USERS

The latest version of Internet Explorer can be downloaded free by going to: **www.microsoft.com** and entering "Internet Explorer" in the Search window. You may also check the "protection-help" section on Suze's Website for a link to this site.

AOL USERS

If you are experiencing difficulties with AOL and the Protection Portfolio CD-ROM, please follow the steps below to load the CD-ROM manually:

1. Open the AOL browser icon , but DO NOT CONNECT TO AOL OR THE INTERNET. You do not need to be connected to use the CD-ROM—but you do need a browser to view the CD-ROM.

2. Go to the "File" menu in the upper left corner.

3. Click on "Open." An "Open a File" window will appear on your screen. Adjacent to the "Look in" box, click on the arrow pointing down.

4. Click on the drive containing the PROTECT CD-ROM. The files found on the CD-ROM will appear. Double-click on "index" or "index.htm," and the CD-ROM will run.

This process should successfully load the Protection Portfolio.

MANUAL INSTALLATION

On a Windows PC:
(1) Insert CD-ROM into computer disk drive.
(2) Choose "Run" from the start menu.
(3) Enter **D:\start.exe** or the drive the CD-ROM is in if in another drive.

On a Macintosh Computer:
(1) Insert CD-ROM into computer disk drive.
(2) Double-click to open CD icon onto desktop.
(3) Double-click on the file **index.htm** to open in your default browser.

Note: If you have problems loading the CD-ROM in either your PC or Macintosh, please open and read the README.TXT file located on you CD-ROM.

SUPPORT

If you have technical-support questions about the Suze Orman Protection Portfolio™ CD-ROM, please see the "protectionhelp" section of Suze Orman's Website at **www.suzeorman.com**. Click on the **protectionhelp** icon at the top of the Website and enter your user name and password (user name: **asksuze**; password: **rajas**). In "protectionhelp," you will find help information including Frequently Asked Questions, as well as an option to send an e-mail to the technical-support staff of the Suze Orman Protection Portfolio for additional assistance.

Table of Contents

SUZE ORMAN'S PROTECTION PORTFOLIO™ CD-ROM FORMS AND WEBSITE LINKS

Credit Report/Card Documents

- Request a Credit Report
- Request Reinvestigation
- Request to Correct Missing Information
- Request Follow-up After Reinvestigation
- Request Removal of Incorrect Information by Creditor
- Credit Verification Form—Phone
- Credit Verification Form—Letter
- www.myfico.com
- www.experian.com
- www.tuc.com
- www.equifax.com

Important Personal Documents

- National Vital Statistics Directory
- Birth Certificate Request
- Application for Passport by Mail, DS-82
- Application for Passport Form, DS-11
- Military Records Request
- U.S. Immigration and Naturalization Services Online Catalog of Forms
- Cohabitation Agreement
- Marriage Certificate Request
- Divorce Decree Request
- Death Certificate Request

Home Ownership Documents

- Real Property Co-Ownership Agreement
- Property Insurance List

Personal Insurance Documents

- How Would a Death Change My Family Expenses
- How Would a Death Change My Family Income
- Where Would We Stand in Case of a Death
- What the Death Benefit of My/My Life Partner's Insurance Policy Needs to Be
- Summary of Life Insurance Needs
- Insurance Rating Services
- Insurance Quoting Services

Social Security Documents

- Social Security Statement Request
- Application for Social Security Card (New, Replacement, or Name Change)

Retirement Plan Documents

- Which Joint and Survivor Benefit Option Might Be Best for You
- Monthly Pension Versus Lump-Sum Payment

Investment Documents

- Cash Accounts
- Mutual Funds, Money Market Accounts, Credit Unions
- Securities Accounts
- Partnerships, Limited Liability Companies, and Joint Ventures
- Individual Retirement Accounts (IRAs) or Pension Plans

Estate Planning Documents

- Advanced Directive and Durable Power of Attorney for Health Care
- www.partnershipforcaring.org
- Financial Power of Attorney
- Will
- Pour Over Will
- Letter to Executor of Will for Tangible Personal Property
- Will Affidavit
- Do I Need a Trust to Avoid Probate
- Revocable Living Trust
- How to Fund the Revocable Trust
- Request to Change Mutual Fund Ownership
- Assignment of Business Interest
- Request to Transfer Stock Ownership
- Assignment of Right to Exercise Stock Option Plan After Death
- Request to Change Bank Account Ownership to Trust
- Request to Change Interest in Limited Partnership to Trust
- Amendment to LLC
- IRA Beneficiary Designation Form
- Final Instructions Form
- What to Do When Someone Dies Checklist
- Restatement of Revocable Living Trust

Protect Yourself

Chapter One

PROTECT YOURSELF

*As I travel around the country, people often say to me, **"Tell me what I need to know to protect my family."** My advice is always the same. In order to protect the ones you love from financial harm in case of your incapacity or unexpected death, you must have a will, a revocable living trust with an incapacity clause, a financial durable power of attorney, an advanced directive and durable power of attorney for health care. You must also take steps to insure that your family members know where all essential documents are stored, including birth certificates, titles and deeds, insurance policies, retirement-plan records, stock certificates, and tax returns.*

Why I Created the Protection Portfolio

To make this process easier for you, I have created the Suze Orman Protection Portfolio™. The Protection Portfolio is a systematic approach to organizing your essential documents, including those mentioned above, and it is very different from anything else out there. Each file folder in the Protection Portfolio system is preprinted with a list of all the documents that I recommend you file there and also with a list of do's and don'ts. I have included two instructional audio CDs, called "What You Need to Know Today to Protect Your Tomorrows™," plus a CD-ROM for your computer. On the two instructional CDs, you will be introduced to Janet Dobrovolny, my own personal trust attorney and someone I consider to be one of the nation's top experts on estate planning. As you listen to the CDs, you will hear Janet and me explaining—clause by clause—the essential documents that we believe everyone must have. On the CD-ROM, you will find the forms you need— forms covering everything from correcting your credit report to leaving final instructions for your funeral. Throughout this guidebook, I will be directing you to go to the Protection Portfolio Forms CD-ROM to print out the appropriate forms to fit your needs.

Once you've completed the forms, I urge you to have an attorney review your completed documents; no book, software program, or other published material—no matter how good—is a substitute for legal advice that pertains to your specific situation.

Inside the back cover of this guidebook, you will find emergency contact cards. Before reading further, please remove one of the emergency cards. Fill in the requested information and insert the card into the plastic pocket on the Portfolio's inside spine. (I have included extra cards in case you make a mistake or your information changes.) If you do not have all the information asked for, fill in the facts you do have and make it a point to obtain the rest of the information within a week. This will ensure that your loved ones know whom to contact in case of an emergency.

Let me add a word about the importance of the Protection Portfolio. When I was seeing clients, I can't tell you how many times a client's husband, wife, adult child, partner, or sibling would come into my office after the client's illness or death, believing that he or she had all the necessary information and had obtained all the pertinent forms and filled them out correctly. Guess what? More often than not, there were mistakes, missing pieces of information, or oversights that created problems. Sometimes, a trust document was filled out incorrectly. Other times, investments that should have been dealt with in a will or trust were undiscovered. By the time my clients' loved ones came to see me, it was often too late to fix a problem.

The Protection Portfolio has been created to ensure that this will never happen to you and your loved ones. Please take the necessary steps today to protect the tomorrows of those you love.

Now Is the Time to Get Rid of Your Financial Clutter

As you go through this guidebook, I will tell you which of your documents you need to keep in the Protection Portfolio. The list won't include all your papers, by any means; the purpose of the Protection Portfolio is not to provide a storage place for every financial record you receive but rather to give you an organized storage system for your most essential documents—those you need to keep safely in one central location in order to protect the people you love.

I'm not suggesting that you throw away your other papers. In a separate place, such as a desk or a filing cabinet, I want you to keep the statements, receipts, and documents you need as a record of your financial transactions for as long as you need them—and you will want to hold on to some of them permanently. (Please see the chart below showing you how long different kinds of documents should be kept.) Yet after a time, many of your papers can be discarded. When discarding them, I would like you to use a shredder. If a shredder is not available, please cut or tear them so that your account numbers and Social Security number are not recognizable.

DOCUMENT	HOW LONG TO KEEP
	One Month
ATM printouts	After you balance your checkbook every month, throw away all ATM receipts.
	One Year
Paycheck stubs	Once you have compared these with your W-2 form and annual Social Security statement, discard.
Medical bills	Keep all your medical records for the entire calendar year, until you file your tax return and can see whether they add up to enough for a deduction; if you take a deduction, keep these records for three years after filing.
Utility bills	Discard after one year, unless you take the cost of utilities as a deduction (for a home office, for example); in that case, keep for three years after filing.
Cancelled checks	Keep for one year, unless needed for tax purposes, in which case keep for three years after filing.
Bank statements	Keep for one year, unless needed for tax purposes, in which case keep for three years after filing.
Credit card receipts	Keep for one year, unless needed for tax purposes, in which case keep for three years after filing.
Quarterly investment statements	Hold on to these until after you have compared them to your annual statement, then discard. Hold your annual statement for three years after the sale of any investment.

DOCUMENT	HOW LONG TO KEEP
	Three Years
Income tax returns, plus documentation, including receipts, cancelled checks, and other documents that support income or a deduction on your tax return	Keep returns for at least three years. Please bear in mind that you can be audited by the IRS for no reason for up to three years after you have filed a tax return, or up to six years if your returns include capital gains or losses, if you own your own business or are self-employed, if you have inherited considerable sums of money or have bought and sold a lot of property. For records that would help you through an audit, a conservative approach is to keep them for seven years. *Also, if you omit 25 percent of your gross income, you can be audited by the IRS for up to six years. If you don't file a tax return at all, there is no statute of limitations. Hold on to your returns, W-2 forms,1099 forms, records of investment income, and/or any other income (rental income, for example), and documentation of tax deductions.*
Cancelled insurance policies	Keep for three years.
Records of selling a house	Keep for three years. You will also need home-sale records as documentation for any capital gains tax.
Home improvement records	Hold for at least three years after filing the tax return that includes the income or loss on the asset (your home) when it's sold.
Record of selling a stock	Keep for at least three years as documentation for any capital gains or capital loss on your tax return.
Annual investment statement	Keep for three years after you sell any investment.
Records of withdrawing	Keep for three years, money from a retirement account.
	Seven Years
Records of satisfied loans	Keep for seven years.
	Keep While Active
Sales receipts	Keep until warranty expires, until you can no longer return or exchange the item purchased, or (if needed for tax purposes) for three years.
Disputed bills	Keep the bill until the dispute has been resolved.
Titles (of home, auto, boat, etc.)	Keep until you sell and transfer title.
Other property records	Keep while active.
Certificates of deposit	Keep until CDs are cashed in.
Stock certificates	Keep while active.

DOCUMENT	HOW LONG TO KEEP
Keep While Active	
Disability insurance policy	Keep while active.
Auto insurance policy	Up to the limit of your state's statute of limitations for liability, in case of late claims.
Homeowner's insurance	Up to the limit of your state's statute of policy limitations for liability, in case of late claims.
Health insurance policy	Keep while active.
Other insurance documents	Keep while active.
Loan agreements	Keep until loan has been fully paid and proof of payment has been received.
Child support orders	Keep until the child reaches age 21.
Contracts	Keep while active.
Retirement plan records	Keep while active; also keep statements.
Keep Forever	
Birth certificate	Keep forever.
Citizenship papers	Keep forever.
Passport	Keep forever.
Marriage certificate	Keep forever.
Domestic partner registration	Keep forever.
Adoption certificate	Keep forever.
Divorce decree	Keep forever.
Death certificate	Keep forever.
Social Security card	Keep forever.
Records of paid mortgages	Keep forever.
Will	Keep forever.
Revocable living trust	Keep forever.
Durable power of attorney	Keep forever.

Your Credit Cards & Records

Chapter Two

YOUR CREDIT CARDS & RECORDS

Please locate and collect the documents listed in the "Credit Reports/Card Documents Checklist" at right and file each document in your Protection Portfolio. Once a document has been filed, check it off on the printed checklist on your file folder.

It's important that you file away a copy of your current credit report and your credit (or FICO) score, as well as photocopies of your active credit cards, in the Protection Portfolio. Why? The reason to keep an up-to-date copy of your credit report—a document that contains vital personal financial information about you—is twofold. First, it's important for you to regularly check your credit report—long before you apply for a mortgage or other loan, say, and find that an error is creating a credit problem. Second, in case of your death, easy access to a current credit report will provide your loved ones with a list of all or most of your outstanding debts. That way, if the need arises for an authorized person to distribute your assets, he or she will have a record of every institution that claims you owe it money.

As to your current credit cards, making a photocopy of both sides of each active credit card and filing the copies in the "Credit" folder of your Protection Portfolio will give you and your loved ones all the information needed to call and cancel or replace your cards in the event that something happens, either to you or to the cards.

How to Get a Copy of Your Credit Report

Your credit report is a compilation of information from the electronic credit file that the major credit bureaus keep on you. It contains

---

CREDIT REPORTS/CARD DOCUMENTS CHECKLIST

❑ Photocopies of your active credit cards, both front and back, with 800 service numbers visible
❑ An up-to-date copy of your credit report and FICO score
❑ Copies of letters closing old credit cards

---

your credit history over the last seven to ten years and includes your address, phone number, Social Security number, past addresses, employment history, marriages and divorces, current credit card accounts and outstanding loans, any history of late payments, any liens or judgments against you, and/or any bankruptcies. Periodically—once every two or three years, if not more often—you should check to make sure that all the information—including any paid-off loans or closed accounts—is current and accurate. If the status of any information in your credit report has changed, replace the old credit report in the Protection Portfolio with the new one.

At your request, a credit bureau must provide you with a copy of the information in your file, along with a list of all parties that have requested it recently. For a nominal fee, typically around $9, you can obtain a copy by phoning, writing, or applying on-line to one of the three major credit bureaus listed below. (On your Protection Portfolio Forms CD-ROM you will find the form **"Request a Credit Report"** already pre-addressed for mailing to the three major credit bureaus as well as a link to request a report on-line.) If you have been turned down for credit on the basis of information supplied by a credit bureau and you request a copy of your credit report within 60 days of receiving notice of that action, you can apply for a free copy through the credit card company or bank that turned you down.

The three big credit bureaus are:

Equifax Credit Information Services, Inc.
P.O. Box 740241
Atlanta, GA 30374
800-685-1111
www.equifax.com

Experian
P.O. Box 2002
Allen, TX 75013
888-EXPERIAN (888-397-3742)
www.experian.com

TransUnion LLC
Consumer Disclosure Center
P.O. Box 1000
Chester, PA 19022
800-888-4213 (to order a copy of your
credit report)
800-916-8800
(to ask a question about your credit report)
www.transunion.com

A Word about Credit Scoring

For an additional fee of about $12, you can usually also get a copy of your credit "score," commonly called a FICO score. I recommend that you do this, and keep a copy in your Protection Portfolio.

Credit scoring is a tool used by lenders in which a numerical value is assigned to a borrower's overall creditworthiness. Here's how it works. Say you apply for a loan or credit. When your application form arrives at the bank or credit card company, an employee enters all the pertinent information from your application into the company computer. The computer then dials up the credit bureau's computer, which assembles your credit report on the spot. The lender's computer analyzes the combined data from your application form and the credit report, and comes up with a numerical FICO "score" that guides the lender in deciding whether to approve a loan or extend you credit.

FICO scores take into account information about your checking and savings account balances and activity, your outstanding debt, and your payment history. Scores range from 350 to 900. The better your record, the higher your score. To be approved for a loan or a line of credit, you want a FICO score of 650 or higher. If your score is below that, you are considered at risk for default. If you score between 620 and 650, you are typically placed in a kind of limbo until you have provided the lender with further documentation. If you want to check your FICO score, you can now do so through the credit bureaus or at *www.myfico.com*, where the cost is $12.95 and includes a copy of your credit report. On your CD-ROM you will find a link to *www.myfico.com* to apply on-line.

How to Correct a Mistake on Your Credit Report

1. Submit a request for reinvestigation. If you find a mistake on your credit report, fill out the "Request for Reinvestigation" form that will accompany your mailed credit report or be offered as an option when you view your credit report on-line. If you do not receive this form in the mail, you can write to the credit bureau and ask for one, or simply open your Protection Portfolio Forms CD-ROM, where you will find the form "**Request Reinvestigation.**" When filling out the form, list each incorrect item and explain how and why it is wrong. Be sure to make and keep a copy of the form before sending it back. Reinvestigations are free. The credit bureau must complete its investigation within 30 days of receiving your complaint (extended to 45 days if the bureau receives additional information from you during the

30-day period).

2. Ask to add missing information. If there is information missing from your credit report that you would like to see included—such as a loan that has been repaid—write a letter asking that this information be added, or simply use the "**Request to Correct Missing Information**" form on your Protection Portfolio Forms CD-ROM.

3. If there is no response to a request for reinvestigation, follow up. If you don't hear from the credit bureau within 30 days, send a follow-up letter using the form that we have supplied on the CD-ROM, "**Request Follow-up After Reinvestigation.**" Send a copy of this form to the Federal Trade Commission, the agency that oversees credit bureaus. Again, keep a copy for your records.

> Federal Trade Commission
> Consumer Response Center CRC-240
> 600 Pennsylvania Ave., NW
> Washington, DC 20580
> 877-FTC-HELP
> (877-382-4357)
> *www.ftc.gov*

4. If the credit bureau will not amend your credit report after the reinvestigation, write to the original creditor. If the credit bureau responds by claiming that the creditor originally reporting the information has verified its accuracy and concluded that the information will remain on your credit report, you will need to take more aggressive action. Send a letter to the creditor associated with the false information and demand that the creditor ask the credit bureau to remove it. (Use the form "**Request Removal of Incorrect Information by Creditor**" on your Protection Portfolio Forms CD-ROM.) If the information was reported by a collection agency, send

the agency a copy of the letter, too. Be sure to keep a copy for your files.

5. If the creditor agrees that the information on your credit report is incorrect, make sure that it is removed. If the creditor agrees that the disputed information is incorrect and should be removed from your file, print the "**Creditor Verification**" form we have supplied and send it to the credit bureau. Include a copy of the creditor's letter acknowledging the error; or, if you spoke by phone to a representative of the creditor company, include that person's name, title, and phone number.

How Long Does Information Stay in My Credit Report?

In most cases, of course, all negative items will eventually be removed from your credit record. Below is a list of how long each kind of information may, by law, remain in your file. If an item remains in your file longer than it should, you can use the "Request Reinvestigation" form that will accompany your mailed credit report (or be offered as an

---

HOW TO FILE A COMPLAINT WITH A CREDIT BUREAU

If you can't obtain a satisfactory correction on mistaken credit report, file a complaint. Credit bureaus have departments to handle consumer complaints about incorrect notations that haven't been removed through the usual reinvestigation process. If your credit report is still not correct after reinvestigation, please contact the credit bureau at one of the following numbers:

Experian	888-397-3742
Trans Union	800-916-8800
Equifax	800-685-1111

How Long Information Stays in Your Credit Report	
Item in credit report	**How long it can remain on file**
Bankruptcies	The record of a bankruptcy may remain on your credit report for no longer than ten years from the date of the last activity in the bankruptcy procedure. (Most credit bureaus start counting the ten-year period from the earlier date of filing.) Please note: Credit bureaus typically report successfully completed Chapter 13 bankruptcies for only seven years.
Lawsuits and judgments	The record of a judgment against you may remain for up to seven years from the date of the judgment, or until your state's statute of limitations has expired, whichever is longer. (Typically, a credit bureau deletes records of lawsuits and judgments after seven years.)
Accounts sent for collection (internally or to a collection agency)	Any record of an account sent for collection may remain on your credit report for up to seven years from the date of last activity.
Accounts charged off	These may remain for up to seven years from the date of last activity.
Paid tax liens	These may remain for up to seven years from the date of last activity.
Criminal records	These may remain for up to seven years from the date of last activity.

option when you view your credit report on-line) to ask that it be deleted.

Statutes of Limitations

A statute of limitation defines the limited period of time during which you can be sued for an act or event you engaged in, such as an auto accident or breaking a contract—including an obligation to pay a debt. Statutes of limitations for credit card debt vary from state to state, but in every state the clock begins to tick from the date you failed to make a payment that was due—that is, as long as you never make another payment on that credit card account. (If you do make another payment, the clock begins to tick all over again; creditors sometimes try to get you to make an additional payment just as the clock is about to run out, so be careful.) For example, if your state's statute on credit card debt is seven years and your last payment was due on January 10, 2000, then the statute of limitations on your debt would run out seven years from that time, on January 10, 2007, assuming you haven't made another payment.

STATUTES OF LIMITATIONS ON CREDIT CARD DEBT BY STATE

Alabama	3 years
Alaska	6 years
Arizona	3 years
Arkansas	3 years
California	4 years
Colorado	6 years
Connecticut	6 years
Delaware	3 years
District of Columbia	3 years
Florida	4 years
Georgia	4 years
Hawaii	6 years
Idaho	4 years
Illinois	5 years
Indiana	6 years
Iowa	5 years
Kansas	3 years
Kentucky	5 years
Louisiana	3 years
Maine	6 years
Maryland	3 years
Massachusetts	6 years
Michigan	6 years
Minnesota	6 years
Mississippi	3 years
Missouri	5 years
Montana	5 years
Nebraska	4 years
Nevada	4 years
New Hampshire	3 years
New Jersey	6 years
New Mexico	4 years
New York	6 years
North Carolina	3 years
North Dakota	6 years
Ohio	—
Oklahoma	3 years
Oregon	6 years
Pennsylvania	6 years
Rhode island	10 years
South Carolina	3 years
South Dakota	6 years
Tennessee	6 years
Texas	4 years
Utah	4 years
Vermont	6 years
Virginia	3 years
Washington	3 years
West Virginia	5 years
Wisconsin	6 years
Wyoming	8 years

NEED TO KNOW

If you apply for credit or insurance worth at least $150,000 or a job that pays $75,000 or more annually, then bankruptcies, lawsuits, paid tax liens, accounts sent out for collection, and criminal records can be reported indefinitely on your credit report. Even in these cases, however, credit bureaus typically delete all items after seven or ten years.

Your Most Important Personal Documents

Chapter Three

YOUR MOST IMPORTANT PERSONAL DOCUMENTS

Please locate and collect the documents listed in the "Important Personal Documents Checklist" at right and file each in your Protection Portfolio. Instructions for ordering copies appear on the following pages. Once a document has been filed, check it off on the printed checklist on your file folder.

If something were to happen to you or a family member on whom you depend, would you or your loved ones know where to find all the important personal documents that might be needed? In case of an emergency, it is critical that your personal documents be stored where both you and those you love can find them.

How to Avoid Identity Theft

Before I tell you which documents to file, I want to take a moment to discuss identity theft, which is a growing problem. The best way to protect yourself against identity theft is to strictly limit the personal information that you make available in any given situation. When you are asked to provide credit card numbers, a Social Security number, a passport number, or any other kind of identifying information, for example, be sure to ask how the information will be used and whether it will be sold to or shared with others. If the answer is yes, request that it be held confidentially; if the vendor refuses, reconsider the transaction you're about to enter into. Here are other safeguards:

1. Look for unauthorized charges on your monthly credit card bills. If you find one, report it immediately to your credit card company.

IMPORTANT PERSONAL DOCUMENTS CHECKLIST

- ❏ Birth certificate(s)
- ❏ Adoption certificate(s)
- ❏ Copy of driver's license(s)
- ❏ Passport(s)
- ❏ Military record of service
- ❏ Citizenship papers and/or green card
- ❏ Cohabitation agreement
- ❏ Prenuptial or postnuptial agreement
- ❏ Marriage certificate
- ❏ Domestic partner registration
- ❏ Child- and/or spousal-support order
- ❏ Divorce decree
- ❏ Death certificate(s)

Once a year, review your credit report to make sure that there has been no suspicious activity.

2. Protect your mail. If you are planning to be away, place a hold on mail by contacting the U.S. Postal Service at 800-275-8777.

3. Place protective passwords on all your accounts. These include credit card, bank, brokerage, and phone accounts. Don't use the same password for all accounts and avoid predictable passwords, such as your birth date, street address, mother's maiden name, or the last four digits of your Social Security number.

4. Limit the amount of personal identification that you carry. This will protect you in case of the loss or theft of your wallet, and especially the number of credit cards.

5. Never reveal identifying numbers over the phone, unless you have initiated the phone transaction.

6. Use a shredder to destroy credit card receipts, bank and brokerage statements, insurance forms, etc.

7. Guard yourself at work. Find out who at the office has access to your personal records and ask that they be kept in a secure location.

8. State your Social Security number only when other types of identification are not accepted. Don't carry your Social Security card in your wallet; leave it in the Protection Portfolio.

If you do have a problem with identity theft, take the following actions.

• *Stolen mail.* If identity theft occurs as a result of someone stealing your mail, contact your local postal inspector or file a complaint on the Postal Service Website at *http://www.usps.com/postalinspectors/fraud/wel come.htm.*

• *Credit card accounts, bank accounts.* Close your account immediately and request that a password be added before any changes can be made to your new account.

• *Investments.* Report the identity theft to your broker or account manager and to the Securities and Exchange Commission. You can file a complaint with the SEC by calling 202-942-7040, by visiting the complaint center at *www.sec.gov/complaint.shtml,* or by writing:

> SEC Office of Investor Education and Assistance
> 450 Fifth Street, NW
> Washington, DC 20549-0213

• *Social Security.* Report theft of your Social Security number to the Social Security Administration's Fraud Hotline at 1-800-269-0271.

Here's how to obtain the documents that should be kept in your Protection Portfolio:

Birth Certificate(s)

If you (and/or your partner or spouse and children) were born in the United States, an official certificate of your (or their) birth can be found on permanent file in the vital statistics office of the state or municipality where you (or they) were born. To request a certified copy, use the **"Birth Certificate Request"** form found on your Protection Portfolio Forms CD-ROM. There, you will also find a link to a national vital statistics directory that lists addresses and fees at: *www.cdc.gov/nchs/howto/w2w/w2welcom.htm.* Send your form with the required fee to the appropriate state or local vital statistics office. (If you were born outside the United States, please consult the U.S.-based consulate of the country in which you were born.)

Adoption Decree(s)

If you have misplaced an adoption decree/ order, request a certified copy from the agency that facilitated the adoption. In some cases, a certified copy may be obtained by contacting the lawyer who executed the adoption order.

Copy of Driver's License(s)

Keep a photocopy of your driver's license— and those of your spouse and/or minor children—in your Protection Portfolio. That way, if your license is lost, you'll have all the information you need to replace it. You can typically apply for renewal or replacement of a driver's license at any county or state department of motor vehicles office. For a listing of motor vehicle offices near you, as well as Internet links to individual state Websites, go to *www.dmv.org* or check the blue pages in your phone book.

Passport(s)

If you, your partner or spouse, or your children are without a current passport and want to travel outside the country, you'll need to obtain one. Even if you're not planning to travel, it's a good idea to have a current passport for identification purposes. U.S. citizens can get or replace passports as described on the next page. (If you are not a U.S. citizen, please contact the U.S.-based consulate of the country in which you hold citizenship.)

Getting a Passport by Mail

If you already have a passport and want to renew it, and if you can answer yes to every one of the following questions, you may apply for passport renewal by mail.

- Do you already have a passport that is not damaged?
- Have you received that passport within the past 15 years?
- Were you over the age of 16 when the passport was issued?
- Do you still have the same name that is listed in that passport, or do you have a certified copy of a court-ordered name change?

If you answered yes to all of the above, then use the **"Application for Passport by Mail, DS-82"** form on your Protection Portfolio Forms CD-ROM and apply by mail. You will also find a link to the **"Application for Passport By Mail"** form at the Website address:

http://travel.state.gov/download_applications.html

Getting a Passport in Person

If you didn't answer yes to all of the questions in the preceding section, you may have to apply for your passport in person. Look at the list of questions below. If you answer yes to any of them, you will have to appear at your local federal passport office.

- Are you applying for a U.S. passport for the first time?
- Was your previous U.S. passport lost, stolen, or damaged?
- Has your previous passport expired and was it issued more than 15 years ago?
- Has your previous passport expired and was it issued when you were under age 16?
- Has your name changed since your passport was issued and are you not in possession of a legal document formally changing your name?
- Are you are a minor child who is 14 years or older?

Most passport offices now require you to make an appointment in advance, so please call ahead of time. To find the passport office nearest to you, check the blue pages of your phone book, call your local post office, or go to *www.travel.state.gov/passport_services.html*.

When you apply in person, you will be asked to fill out an **"Application for Passport, Form DS-11."** On your Protection Portfolio Forms CD-ROM we have included a link to the "Application for Passport" form at *http://travel.state.gov/download_applications.html.*

For detailed information on applying for a passport or getting a replacement passport, please visit *http://travel.state.gov/download_applications.html.*

Military Record of Service

A form called "report of separation" is needed to verify a history of military service so that you or your loved ones can receive benefits. On request, "Report of Separation" may be sent to a veteran, a deceased veteran's next of kin, or other authorized persons or organizations. The average turnaround time on requests is currently 14 to 16 weeks, so don't put this off. On your Protection Portfolio Forms CD-ROM, there is a link to the **"Military Records Request"** form at *www.archives.gov/facilities/mo/st_louis/military_personnel_records/standard_form_180.html*

Citizenship Papers and/or Green Card

If you have misplaced your citizenship papers, or need to have a revision made, please contact the U.S. Immigration and Naturalization Service (INS). To locate the INS local field office nearest to you, see the blue pages of your phone book or log onto the INS Website at *www.ins.usdoj.gov;* the Website contains local office listings, official forms, 800 numbers for customer service, and a section on most frequently asked questions. For a link to the INS on-line catalog of forms most commonly used to apply, revise, or petition for benefits offered by the INS (*www.ins.usdoj.gov/graphics/formsfee/forms/index.htm*); see the **"Important Personal Documents"** section of your Protection Portfolio Forms CD-ROM. Please note that many INS forms require the payment of a processing fee.

As to a lost or stolen green card, if you are a permanent resident or a conditional resident who needs to replace a card, you can apply for a replacement card by filing a Form I-90: Replace Permanent Resident Card. Form I-90 can also be ordered by calling the INS Forms request line at 800-870-3676 or by downloading the form from the INS Website *www.ins.usdoj.gov.* Unless otherwise instructed, you should file the application (with supporting documentation and fees) in person at your local INS office. If you are outside the U.S. and have lost your green card, contact the nearest American consulate, INS office, or Port of Entry.

Cohabitation Agreement

If you are living with a partner (or planning to live with a partner) to whom you are not married, you may want to consider a cohabitation agreement. This is a must for same-sex couples as well. A cohabitation agreement is a written contract that sets forth your mutual rights and obligations with respect to joint and separate property, as well as stating any other financial or general obligations or expectations you wish to agree upon in advance of (or even after) moving in together. Enforceability of cohabitation agreements varies by state; in some states, only written agreements are honored, and in others the law is unclear as to whether any such agreements will be honored. Still, because negotiating a cohabitation agreement is an oppor-

tunity to state your expectations of each other, I recommend doing this early on. You and your partner can draft a cohabitation agreement yourselves, but be sure to have separate attorneys review it. If you have misplaced your cohabitation agreement, call your attorney, who should have a copy on file. To learn more about cohabitation agreements, please consult attorneys Frederick Hertz, Toni Ihara, and Ralph Warner's book, *Living Together: A Legal Guide for Unmarried Couples;* or attorneys Denis Clifford, Frederick Hertz, and Hayden Curry's *A Legal Guide for Lesbian & Gay Couples;* or log onto *www.nolo.com* for information on ordering these books. On your Protection Portfolio CD-ROM, I have included a cohabitation agreement for your use, prepared by attorney Frederick Hertz.

Prenuptial Agreement

A prenuptial—or premarital or antemarital—agreement is a legal contract entered into before marriage. It describes how your partner's and your assets and debts are to be divided in case of a divorce. A prenup can also record certain non-financial expectations you and your partner bring to the marriage—for example, which partner will work, which partner will stay at home with the children, and various inheritance rights. I think of prenups as an opportunity to discuss marital finances thoroughly before you take your vows and as the best way to ensure your financial security by protecting future earnings or inheritance or shielding against future debts by a spouse who proves financially unstable. Ultimately, a well-written prenup can protect you no matter what financial circumstances may arise. If you have misplaced your prenuptial agreement document, call your attorney, who should have a copy on file.

Postnuptial Agreement

A postnuptial agreement is a legal contract entered into after marriage. Like a prenup, it describes how your and your partner's assets and debts are to be divided in case of a divorce and can also specify non-financial expectations, including various inheritance rights. Unlike prenups, which are now widely accepted by the courts, the enforceability of postnups varies from state to state. If you have misplaced your postnuptial agreement document, call your attorney, who should have a copy on file.

Marriage Certificate

If you were married in the U.S., you can obtain a certified copy of your marriage certificate by sending the **"Marriage Certificate Request"** form and the appropriate fee to the state or local vital statistics office where your marriage occurred. On your Protection Portfolio Forms CD-ROM, you will find a link to: *www.cdc.gov/nchs/howto/w2w/w2welcom.htm,* a national vital statistics directory, which lists addresses and fees. For those married outside the U.S., contact the U.S.-based consulate of the country in which you were married.

Domestic Partner Registration

A number of cities (currently, about 100) allow unmarried couples (same sex and opposite sex) to register as domestic partners and to become eligible for domestic partnership benefits that companies may offer to their employees. Counties, private companies, organizations, universities, and a few state governments (including those of Delaware, Massachusetts, New York, Oregon, and Vermont) provide domestic partner benefits to employees. There are only about 100 towns, cities, and states that currently have domestic partner registries. For a list, visit the Human Rights Campaign Website: *www.hrc.org.*

Child- and/or Spousal-Support Order

If there are children involved when you and your spouse decide to separate or divorce, one of you may need to file a request for temporary child and/or spousal support or alimony, for custody and visitation rights— or for anything else that may apply to your situation—with the local court handling your divorce. Typically, soon after filing you will receive a temporary order from the court; a permanent order will be issued once your divorce is final. Even after a final order has been issued, the court usually has the right to alter child-support provisions until the children are "emancipated," i.e., turn 18 or, if they have not yet graduated from high school, turn 19, whichever comes first. Either ex-spouse can petition the court for a change in support payments or custody arrangements until that time. The court also retains jurisdiction over spousal support until support is terminated.

If you do not have a copy of your child- and/or spousal-support order, please request one. The courthouse where your order was executed will have a copy on file.

Divorce Decree

You can obtain a copy of your divorce decree by sending a **"Divorce Decree Request"** form and the appropriate fee to the state or local vital statistics office where your divorce occurred. On your Protection Portfolio Form CD-ROM, you will find a link to *www.cdc.gov/nchs/howto/w2w/w2welcom.htm,* a national vital statistics directory that lists addresses and fees.

Death Certificate

You can obtain a copy of a death certificate by sending a **"Death Certificate Request"** form and the appropriate fee to the state or local vital statistics office where the death occurred. On your Protection Portfolio Form CD-ROM, you will find a link to *www.cdc.gov/nchs/howto/w2w/w2welcom.htm,* a national vital statistics directory that lists addresses and fees.

Records of Home Ownership
Chapter Four

RECORDS OF HOME OWNERSHIP

Please locate and collect the documents listed in the "Home Ownership Documents Checklist" at right and file each document in your Protection Portfolio. Once a document has been filed, check it off on the printed checklist on your file folder.

Your home is one of your family's most significant resources, both emotionally and financially. Your home is not only where you live and raise your family, but is also probably one of your largest assets and, if anything were to happen to you, a major part of your plan to protect your loved ones. In order to plan ahead as well as possible, please read the following information about taking title to your home, the deeds you may have, and home insurance, and make sure that all your important home ownership documents—deeds, mortgages and other promissory notes, and insurance policies—are safely filed in your Protection Portfolio.

Taking Title

When you buy a piece of property, the way you take title—that is, the way ownership is recorded on the deed—is very important. There are five main variations on how you can take title to a home: as an individual, as joint tenants with right of survivorship, as tenants in common, as tenants by the entirety, and as community property. The way you take title affects your will, living trust, estate tax, income tax, and possibly property tax, so if you are in doubt as to whether you have taken title correctly for your situation, please consult an attorney.

To determine how you took title, check your grant deed (the deed you received when you bought your home; for more information, see the section on "Kinds of Deeds" on pages 32–33). Following are brief descriptions of major ways of taking title to your home.

Individual

If you hold title to your property as an individual, you are the sole owner. The property is yours to dispose of as you choose.

Joint tenancy with right of survivorship (JTWROS)

Joint tenancy with right of survivorship allows two or more people to hold the title to a home. If one person dies, the ownership immediately transfers to the name of the other joint tenant or tenants, without having to go through probate, the court procedure by which assets pass from a deceased person to beneficiaries named in a will. In states that aren't community-property states, married couples are usually (but not always) best off when they take title to a house by JTWROS.

A potential problem with joint tenancy with right of survivorship, though, is that it will override any provisions in your will or living trust. There are good reasons for you to hold your home in joint tenancy, but trying to use it as a substitute for a will (or a trust) is not one of them. And if you want to leave your share of your home to someone other than your spouse (such as a child, for example), joint tenancy with right survivorship is not the way to go.

Tenancy by the entirety

About 30 states allow you and your spouse to hold real estate in tenancy by the entirety,

---

HOME OWNERSHIP DOCUMENTS CHECKLIST

☐ Deeds
☐ Promissory notes
☐ Property co-ownership agreement
☐ Homeowner's insurance
☐ Copy of land survey
☐ Copy of title policy
☐ Most recent property tax bill
☐ Appraisals and evaluation of valuable items such as jewelry, art, and antiques
☐ Fire insurance
☐ Copy of property list in case of loss

which means that neither one of you can transfer the property while you are alive without the other's permission. This is because, under tenancy by the entirety, each of you owns the entire property. Only real estate can be held in this type of tenancy, and only by legally married couples.

NEED TO KNOW
How do you hold title to your home?

Please check off the way in which you hold title to your property. If you don't know the answer, check your deed.

I hold title to my property as
❑ Individual
❑ Joint tenancy with right to survivorship
❑ Tenants in common
❑ Tenancy by the entirety
❑ Community property

Tenancy in common (TIC)

When property is held as tenants in common, it is owned by two or more individuals who each hold an undivided proportionate interest in the property. Each person can own a different percentage of the property. Anything owned as a tenant in common is subject to probate, unless shares in the property are transferred into a living trust, in which case probate can be avoided.

Community property

Eight states (Arizona, California, Idaho, Louisiana, Nevada, New Mexico, Texas, and Washington) have community-property laws, which create a particular form of co-ownership for married couples. Wisconsin has a similar property system, though there community property is called "marital property." While the laws in each of these states are different, as a general rule community- and marital-property states hold that the income and property acquired by a married couple should be divided equally in the event of a divorce, unless both spouses agree in writing to an alternate arrangement. Thus, in a community- or marital-property state, all "marital" property is owned by you and your spouse equally, where "marital" property includes everything acquired during the course of the marriage other than by gift or inheritance.

In community- and marital-property states, when one spouse dies, 100 percent of a marital asset (such as a house bought after marriage) is given a new tax basis equal to the date-of-death value of the asset. This can represent a tremendous tax savings to the surviving spouse if he or she sells the asset. To get this benefit, however, you must be sure the title includes the wording "as community property" when taking title to your home.

Please note: Five of the nine community property states—Arizona, California, Nevada, Texas, and Wisconsin—let couples add the right of survivorship to community property, permitting you to bypass probate and transfer title automatically at death. The only drawback: If both partners die simultaneously, the property goes to probate.

TEST YOURSELF
Do you hold title to your home in the best possible way for you?

According to your state and marital status, is there a more advantageous way you could hold title to your property?

❑ YES   ❑ NO

If you answered yes, please contact a title company and change how you hold title to your home. In almost all cases, title to your home should be held in a living trust.

Kinds of Deeds

Now that you know how to take title to your home, it's important that you know the difference between deeds that you may have now or in the future. There are three kinds of deeds that you may encounter. For each kind that applies to you, please keep a copy in your Protection Portfolio.

A grant deed, or warranty deed, shows that you purchased your home and that the title was legally transferred to you.

A deed of trust is the kind of deed that shows you owe money to a bank or other lender and that you have secured the loan with your property; this is the kind of deed you sign when you take out a mortgage. The amount of money you've borrowed and the terms of the loan are contained in a signed **promissory note,** which you should have, and keep a copy.

A deed of reconveyance shows that the lender has been repaid and has reconveyed its security interest in the property back to you.

Homeowner's Insurance

When you purchased your home, the lending institution that issued your mortgage probably required that you get homeowner's insurance; if so, you should have an insurance contract that spells out your policy's terms and conditions, as well as your level of coverage. Please locate it, but before you file it in the Protection Portfolio, check to be sure that you have adequate insurance.

What's adequate for your needs? Standard policies have two parts. The first part of your policy should cover the total cost of rebuilding, repairing, or replacing your home, property, and/or personal belongings, such as furniture and valuables, in case of burglary or a disaster, such as a fire or storm. The second part should cover liability for any injuries or damage that you or your family might cause to other people. One item to check on is whether you have enough insurance on your personal possessions. Your policy should cover the replacement value—not the cash value—of these belongings. Also, be aware that standard policies put a cap on coverage of your belongings—typically, between 50 percent and 70 percent of the amount of your policy. If this is not enough, consider additional coverage. Finally, most policies come with liability coverage that ranges from $100,000 to $300,000. If this is not enough, consider what's called an umbrella policy. It sits "on top" of your policy and provides extra coverage—up to $1 million or more.

Fire Insurance

Your homeowner's insurance nominally covers the cost of repairing or rebuilding your home if it is damaged in a fire, but depending on the restrictions in your policy, that coverage may not be enough to restore your home to its pre-fire condition. If that's the case, consider buying additional insurance.

Other Documents to Store

• *Property co-ownership agreement:* A property co-ownership agreement details how your property is owned and can be bought out by a co-owner. This type of agreement is important if you co-own property as part of an unmarried couple or if you are buying a property (such as a duplex) with a friend. On your Protection Portfolio CD-ROM you will find a **"Real Property Co-Ownership Agreement"** prepared by attorney Frederick Hertz. To learn more about real property co-ownership agreements, please consult attorneys Frederick Hertz, Toni Ihara, and Ralph Warner's book, *Living Together: A Legal Guide for Unmarried Couples;* or attorneys Denis Clifford, Frederick Hertz, and Hayden Curry's *A Legal Guide for Lesbian & Gay Couples;* or log onto *www.nolo.com* for information on ordering these books.

• *Copy of land survey:* A basic land survey verifies the boundaries of your property. Keep it in your Protection Portfolio.

• *Copy of title policy:* Title insurance is required by most mortgage companies to ensure there isn't a lien against the title, or the seller of the property really owns it. File it in your Protection Portfolio.

• *Copy of property list in case of loss:* On the next page and on your CD-ROM, you will find a form to list your personal property. If you suffer a loss due to theft, fire, flood, wind or other disaster, you will need to supply this list to your insurance provider.

PROPERTY LIST IN CASE OF LOSS DUE TO THEFT, FIRE, FLOOD, WIND, OR OTHER DISASTER

Please attach copies of receipts, cancelled checks, proof of purchases, warranties, appraisals, and any pictures for the items listed below.

Description of item	Brand Name	Manufacturer	Model #	Place of Purchase (store and location)	Date Purchased (if gift or inheritance, give date or age of item)	Cost of Item Including Sales Tax, Shipping & Handling (if applicable)	Receipt, Cancelled Check, or Proof of Purchase Attached (Yes or No)	Warranty Attached (Yes or No)	Appraisal Attached (Yes or No)	Picture Attached (Yes or No)

Documents about Automobiles, Recreational Vehicles & Boats

Chapter Five

AUTOMOBILES, RECREATIONAL VEHICLES & BOATS

Please locate and collect the documents listed in the "Automobile, Recreational Vehicle, & Boat Documents Checklist" at right and file each document in your Protection Portfolio.

Why You Need to Keep Your Auto-, RV-, and Boat-Ownership Documents Safe and Sound

Just as it is important to keep safe the deed and mortgage to your home, it's important to keep the ownership and loan records of your cars, trucks, recreational vehicles, boats—even your airplane, if you own one!—in your Protection Portfolio, so that you and your loved ones know exactly where the records of these assets and liabilities are. It's also important to file all your insurance policies—also important assets, especially in the event of an accident, theft, or other insured event. I'll say more about insurance records in the section on "Personal Insurance."

How to Protect Yourself When You Sell a Car, Boat, or Recreational Vehicle

The most important thing to remember when transferring ownership of a car, boat, or RV is not to give the buyer physical possession of the car until you have received a copy of the new registration from the department of motor vehicles showing the new owner on title. That way, you won't be liable in case of an accident or other mishap after the vehicle leaves your possession.

How Much Car Insurance You Need

If you own a car or truck, you are required to carry certain types of coverage by the state you live in and—if you borrowed money to buy your car—by the lending institution that gave you your loan. Basic policies usually include some combination of liability, colli-

---

AUTOMOBILE, RECREATIONAL VEHICLE, & BOAT DOCUMENTS CHECKLIST

- ❑ Automobile titles and/or leases
- ❑ Automobile insurance policies
- ❑ Automobile loan documents
- ❑ Recreational vehicles titles
- ❑ Recreational vehicles insurance policies
- ❑ Recreational vehicles loan documents
- ❑ Boat titles
- ❑ Boat insurance policies
- ❑ Boat loan documents

---

sion, comprehensive, uninsured or underinsured motorist, and medical payments coverage.

As for the level of coverage you need, consider your personal situation. Answer the following questions and think about what will make you feel safe.

- Is your car brand new or a few years old?
- How much would it cost you to replace your car?
- Do you have the resources to pay for medical bills and car repairs?
- Do you have valuable assets you want to protect?

After answering these questions, if you feel you do not have adequate insurance, contact your insurance provider and discuss increasing your coverage.

How to Reduce Auto Insurance costs

The premiums on your car insurance are based on your age, your sex, where you live, the type of car you drive, and your driving record, among other things. Most policies give discounts for:

- ❑ A clean driving record, with no points on your license
- ❑ Preferred age, sex, and marital status (typically, single women over age 25, single men over age 30, and married women of any age)

❑ Good grades in high school, college, or even graduate school
❑ A car supplied with air bags, antilock brakes, or an alarm system
❑ Multiple cars in your household

These discounts may seem arbitrary, but they aren't. The qualifications mentioned are statistically correlated with drivers who have fewer accidents. Make it a point to see if your family qualifies for any of these discounts with your insurance provider.

Insurance for Recreational Vehicles

Insurance for RVs is not the same as standard auto insurance. The value of the vehicle and the potential for damage in the event of an accident mean that ordinary auto insurance minimums are too low. You may be able to get a policy with higher limits from your regular auto insurance provider, but probably not; most auto insurance providers do not cover RVs. So if you are planning to buy an RV, you will have to do some homework to find an insurance provider. For more information, please visit the Website *www.insure.com.*

Insurance for Boats

Boats are easier to insure than RVs, but to find a good policy you must still do some research. Your homeowner's insurance may include coverage for watercraft, but such coverage is typically very limited. If you are a prospective boat owner and plan on docking your boat in a marina, you will probably want to explore a separate watercraft policy or rider with your insurance provider. The insurance industry separates watercraft into the following categories:

❑ Boats (usually from 16 feet to 25 feet 11 inches long)
❑ Yachts (26 feet or larger)
❑ Personal watercraft (jet skis, wave runners, other personal watercraft)

The cost of the policy will be dictated by the type of boat, size, age of boat, where it will be used, and the skill level and age of the operator (you).

Personal Insurance Policies & Records

Chapter Six

PERSONAL INSURANCE POLICIES & RECORDS

Please locate and collect the documents listed in the "Personal Insurance Documents Checklist" at right and file each document in your Protection Portfolio. Once a document has been filed, check it off on the printed checklist on your file folder.

Keeping Your Policies Safe

It is important for you and your loved ones to know exactly where all the documents relating to your personal insurance policies are—including your life insurance, health insurance, Medicare insurance, Medigap or managed-care-organization insurance, Medicaid, long-term-care insurance, and/or long-term disability insurance.

These policies are vital protections in case of illness, accident, incapacity, or death, and your policy documents contain information defining your rights and the insurance company's obligations with respect to your coverage. Your survivors will need to be able to find them, of course, but you may also need to refer to them from time to time. Before making a claim, for example, you will want to check and see what language the policy uses so that you can frame your claim in the appropriate way. Also, if you need to have a lawyer intervene, having your policy on hand can speed things up, because the lawyer won't have to wait to get the policy from the company, which can take anywhere from a few days to weeks.

The Importance of Life Insurance

All your personal insurance is important, but I especially want to say a few words about life insurance because a) life insurance can be a key element in protecting your family's financial future if you and your family are still relatively young; and b) too many people misunderstand the real purpose and function

---

PERSONAL INSURANCE DOCUMENTS CHECKLIST

❑ Life insurance policy, plus notations as to any loans, mortgages, or credit card contracts that carry life insurance
❑ Health insurance card and benefits description
❑ Medicare card and benefits description
❑ Medigap/managed-care-organization policy
❑ Medicaid card and benefits description
❑ Long-term care policy
❑ Long-term disability policy

---

of life insurance and hold on to it (and continue to pay a high price for it) far beyond its usefulness. So let's take a good, hard look at your life insurance needs.

When most people think about the financial security of family members and other loved ones after they are gone, the first thing they think about is life insurance. What's interesting about this is that life insurance was never meant to be a permanent need. Its original purpose was to protect young families that were just starting out, before they'd built up a nest egg, so that if the family breadwinner died early and unexpectedly, the life insurance benefit would keep the family going. If the breadwinner lived his or her life according to plan, however, the family would accumulate enough assets to make the life insurance unnecessary and obsolete.

Today, a huge industry exists to sell you as much insurance as it can, for as long as you live, whether you need it or not. Commissions on life insurance policies, such as whole-life policies, are incredibly lucrative for salespeople, often amounting to 80-90 percent of your first year's premium.

Life insurance should not be seen as a universal financial-planning tool, a way to create a financial legacy for your family, or a safe haven for your savings. There are better places to save money for your future and to accumulate money to pass on to your heirs. Life insurance should be seen as a way to replace lost income if that income cannot be replaced by income from your savings and investments.

Who Does and Doesn't Need Life Insurance, and How Much Is Enough

If you're single and have no dependents, there is no need for you to have life insurance. If you have loved ones who depend on the money you bring in with each and every paycheck, then you do need to consider life insurance.

Below are five steps to take to help you decide whether you should have life insurance and, if so, how much. These steps are based on the premise that, if anything were to happen to you and/or your life partner, you would want your loved ones (or yourself, in the case of the death of a life partner) to have enough money to be able continue to live in exactly the manner in which they (or you) live right now.

1. Figure out whether you and/or your life partner should have life insurance. The first thing you need to do is take the time to figure out how your income and expenses would change if either you or your life partner were to die. Using the worksheets on the following pages, figure out how your family budget would be different if one of you were to die. You will also find these worksheets on the Protection Portfolio Forms CD-ROM with a built-in calculator to make this process as easy as possible.

Using the **"How Would a Death Change My Family Expenses?"** worksheet, reflect on how your family expenses would change if one or the other of you were do die. Most of your fixed household expenses would probably remain the same, since you would still have pay the mortgage, send in property taxes, pay for gas and electricity, pay for homeowner's insurance, etc. But other kinds of expenses (clothing, food, medical expenses, auto, etc.) might increase or decrease. Write down the yearly total in each category for both you and your partner, and then record the overall yearly total for you and your partner.

Next, on the **"How Would a Death Change My Family Income?"** worksheet found on both page 44 and on your Protection Portfolio Forms CD-ROM (which includes a built-in calculator), add up the amount of income you would still have coming in if either you or your partner were no longer able to earn and contribute to the family budget.

While you're thinking about possible changes in your expenses, take some time to consider how your children's suddenly being without one or both parents would affect the family's financial situation.

For example:

❑ Would the remaining partner have to go to work? Would that increase child-care costs?
❑ Could the remaining partner's income cover the financial goals you've set for your children's future—paying for their education, for example?

When you've completed these worksheets, look on page 44 for further instructions.

Now that you've know how your family's income and expenses would be affected if you or your life partner were to die, it is time to figure out where, overall, your family would stand financially. How much would it really take for the family to live? How much do you really have?

From the **"How Would a Death Change My Family Income?"** worksheet, copy your total yearly income and your life partner/spouse's total yearly income into the box on page 45. (This worksheet is also on the Protection Portfolio Forms CD-ROM.)

From the **"How Would a Death Change My Family Expenses?"** worksheet, copy your total yearly expenses and your life partner/spouse's total yearly expenses into the box on

How Would a Death Change My Family Expenses?

	My Yearly Expenses	My Life Partner's Yearly Expenses
Mortgage/rent		
Property taxes		
Home maintenance/ condo fees		
Home insurance		
Gas & electric		
Water		
Garbage removal		
Telephone/cell phone		
Burglar alarm		
House cleaner		
Gardening		
Food		
Medical/dental/ optometric		
Veterinarian		
Insurance		
Auto expenses		
Tolls/parking/ transportation		
Clothes/shoes		
Dry cleaning		
Hair/manicure/facial		
Alimony/child support		
Kids' school		
Job training/education		
Income taxes		
Legal/accounting fees		
Safe-deposit box		
Computers		
Credit cards/loans		
Bank/credit union fees		
Express mail/postage		
Books/subscriptions		
Entertainment/video rentals		
Cable TV		
Sporting events		
Vacations		
Hobbies		
Donations		
Gifts		
Miscellaneous		
TOTAL	$	$

How Would a Death Change My Family Income?

	My Yearly Income	My Life Partner's Yearly Income
Predictable bonuses		
Alimony/child support		
Disability income		
Bond/interest income		
Interest income		
Dividend income		
Yearly paychecks (after taxes/deductions)		
Rental income		
Gifts from parents (if you can count on them)		
Loan repayments		
Pension income		
IRA income		
Miscellaneous		
TOTAL	$	$

page 45. (This worksheet is also on the Protection Portfolio Forms CD-ROM, which includes a built-in calculator.)

Subtract your yearly expenses from your yearly income to determine your deficit or excess. Then subtract your life partner's yearly expenses from his or her yearly income to determine his or her deficit or excess.

Please answer yes or no to the following:

	YES	NO
Do you, or does your life partner, have a deficit?	❏	❏
If either you or your life partner were to die, would the survivor be unable to maintain the household expenses without going into debt?	❏	❏
If either you or your life partner were to die, would the survivor be unable to achieve your financial goals for your family?	❏	❏

If you answered no to all of the above, then you do not need life insurance. You may want some for peace of mind, but you do not need it—and there is a big difference between needing and wanting life insurance.

If you answered yes to any of the questions above, then you do need life insurance to protect yourself and your loved ones.

2. Figure out how much life insurance you and/or your life partner should have. Now that you know you need life insurance, your goal will be to buy enough coverage so that the amount you get in case of death creates the income needed to make up for your family's income deficit. In other words, you want your beneficiaries to be able to live off the income generated by the death benefit without dipping into the principal. The principal should continue to generate income indefinitely, as long as your survivors spend only the interest.

With this in mind, and as a rule of thumb, I would figure on needing about $120,000 in insurance for every $500 of monthly income your family will require.

Let's say, for example, that your household needs $3,000 a month to cover all expenses and income taxes, and that your worst-case scenario is that the survivors in your family will have no wages or other income—they will need the full $3,000. To figure out how much insurance you'll need, you would divide $3,000 by $500 and get a factor of 6; in this case, your insurance policy should be 6 times $120,000, or $720,000 worth of insurance coverage.

Now let's calculate how much projected monthly insurance income you or your life partner may need. In the worksheet **"Monthly Insurance Income Needed"** on the top of the next page, copy the "Difference (deficit)" figure for you and your life partner from the **"Where Would We Stand in Case of a Death?"** worksheet below. Divide by 12 to come up with the projected monthly insurance income needed. (Both of these worksheets are also found on the Protection Portfolio Forms CD-ROM on the **"Where Would We Stand in Case of a Death?"** worksheet.)

Now take the **"Monthly Insurance**

Income Needed" for you and your life partners and plug those figures into the chart on the top of the next page to find out what the death benefit on your/your life partner's insurance policy should be.

3. *Estimate how long you and/or your life partner will need life insurance.* Remember, life insurance was never intended to fill a permanent need. As the years go by, the money you are putting away in retirement accounts, the money you may accumulate on your own, and the decreasing size of your mortgage will probably diminish or even eliminate your need for a life insurance death benefit. Bottom-line goal: By the time you are retired, your need for life insurance—and the necessity to pay premiums on a policy—should be gone. If you have children, you may want to continue to carry some life insurance to provide for them into early adulthood—typically, until your youngest child is 24. By that time, if anything unexpected were to happen to you, your children should be able to support themselves.

Please note: Whatever your circumstances, never, never cancel or attempt to change a life insurance policy without undergoing a thorough physical exam. If there's a medical reason to keep your insurance, you may decide to keep a policy you otherwise would not need.

That said, please estimate how many

Where Would We Stand in Case of a Death?

My Yearly Income	$_____	Partner's Yearly Income	$_____
	minus (—)		minus (—)
My Yearly Expenses	$_____	Partner's Yearly Expenses	$_____
Difference (yearly deficit or excess)	$_____	**Difference** (yearly deficit or excess)	$_____

Monthly Insurance Income Needed		
My Deficit	$_____ divided by 12 = $_____	**Monthly Insurance Income Needed**
Partner's Deficit	$_____ divided by 12 = $_____	**Monthly Insurance Income Needed**

years you and/or your life partner will need life insurance. Write your estimates in the spaces following:

> I will need life insurance for_____ years.
> My life partner will need life insurance for_____ years.

4. Decide what kind of life insurance you and/or your life partner should purchase. In my opinion, there is only one kind of life insurance that makes sense for the vast majority of us, and that is term life insurance. Term insurance is the simplest kind of insurance you can buy, a just-in-case policy that offers the promise of a death benefit for the finite length of time for which you need protection. Term policies are not very expensive, because the insurance company knows that you have relatively little chance of dying—and there-

fore of triggering the payment of a death benefit—while the policy is in force.

By contrast, with whole-life or universal insurance you are expected to keep the policy for the rest of your life and to die with it, so the insurance company knows it will almost certainly have to pay the death benefit. The company sets its premium accordingly. While it's true that whole-life and universal policies accrue cash value and that, if you decide not to keep your policy or suddenly need money, you can cash out at the policy's cash value, it's also true that there are much better ways to save for your future financial needs. Commissions on whole-life policies are some of the most lucrative commissions any-where—and you are paying them. If your goal is to put money aside, you'll be much better off dollar-cost averaging into a good no-load

What the Death Benefit on My and My Life Partner's Insurance Policy Needs to Be		
	Income I Need	**Income My Life Partner Needs**
Projected deficit/monthly insurance income needed is A:	A $_____	A $_____
Divide A by $500 to get B:	B $_____	B $_____
Multiply B by $120,000 to get C:	C $_____	C $_____
C is the amount of death benefit you need in an insurance policy.		

My Life Insurance Summary

Do I need it?
(page 45)   Yes___ No___

How much do I need?
(page 46)   _____

How long will I need it?
(page 46)   _____

What kind of insurance policy do I need?
_____term_____

My Life Partner's Life Insurance Summary

Do I need it?
(page 45)   Yes___ No___

How much do I need?
(page 46)   _____

How long will I need it?
(page 46)   _____

What kind of insurance policy do I need?
_____term_____

mutual fund. If your goal is to ensure that your loved ones will have enough to live on in case of your unexpected death, low-cost term insurance is almost certainly the way to go. Decide for yourself by looking at the chart on the next page.

5. Summarize your life insurance needs. Answer the following questions to make a final decision as to whether you and/or your life partner need life insurance and, if so, how much and for how long.

How to Buy Term Life Insurance

If you have decided you need life insurance, please use one of the insurance quoting services listed on the CD-ROM; my Website, *www.suzeorman.com;* or on this page to find a company and a policy that appears to suit your needs. (While comparison shopping, be prepared to provide information including your sex, date of birth, condition of health, how much insurance, and how long it is needed.) If you already have insurance, use one of these services to compare prices and see if you can get a better deal.

That said, the cheapest policy is not always the best one for you, because you should not simply be comparing price—you should also be comparing a company's financial health, resources, and services. Please don't buy a policy from any company until you check the company with at least two insurance rating services. Call or log on to the rating services' Websites and check the current ratings of the insurance companies you are interested in buying from. The rating you are looking for is either A+ or better or AA or better.

Insurance Quoting Services:

AccuQuote
800-442-9899
www.accuquote.com

Quotesmith
800-556-9393
www.quotesmith.com

InsuranceQuote Services
800-972-1104
www.iquote.com

Select Quote
800-343-1985
www.selectquote.com

InsWeb
800-871-5075
www.insweb.com

TermQuote
800-444-8376
www.termquote.com

MasterQuote
800-337-5433
www.masterquote.com

Insurance Rating Services:

A.M. Best
908-439-2220
www.ambest.com

Standard & Poor's
212-438-2000
www.standardpoor.com

Duff & Phelps
312-263-2610
www.fitchratings.com

Weiss Ratings
407-627-3300 (in Florida)
800-298-8100
www.weissratings.com

Moody's
212-553-0377
www.moodys.com

Compare and Contrast: Term Versus Whole-life Insurance		
	Term Life Insurance	**Whole-life Insurance**
How long is the policy in effect?	Term life insurance remains in effect for a specific period of time—its "term." You can choose a term of anywhere from 1 to 5 to 10 to 20 years.	As long as you pay the premium, whole-life insurance guarantees a death benefit from the moment you buy the policy until you die.
How much does a policy cost?	Term insurance is by far the more cost-effective option. Your annual premium is based on the length of term you choose, plus your age and health at the time you apply for coverage. For example, if you were a healthy, nonsmoking 40-year-old man, a 20-year term life policy with a $300,000 death benefit would cost you about $42 a month.	With whole-life insurance, the insurer can be pretty sure that the policy will be in force when you die and that the company will have to pay out a death benefit, so whole life is more expensive than term. If you were a healthy, nonsmoking 40-year-old man, for example, a whole life policy with a $300,000 death benefit would cost you about $338.64 a month.
What if I decide not to keep or renew the policy?	With term insurance, there is no cash value, so there is no payment due to you if you decide to cancel. If you wish to renew your policy when the term runs out, you have to reapply, In most cases the policy can be renewed but will be priced according to your age, health, and the term at time of renewal. The older you are, the higher the cost, because you are closer to your statistically probable age of death. The cost to renew a term policy for someone in his or her 70s or 80s would very likely be prohibitive.	A whole-life policy has a cash value, so if you decide not to keep the policy or suddenly need money, you can cash out the policy at its cash value. But buyer beware: Commissions on whole-life insurance policies are high, so you might find that the cash value of your insurance is far less than you expected.

Your Health Insurance

In recent years, private health insurance has become an increasingly complex, expensive, and necessary item for all of us. No matter what your age or state of health, protecting yourself and your family with adequate health insurance is an act of self-respect. Please find and keep your health insurance plan rulebook, along with a copy of your plan number, your insurance card, and your primary physician's name, in your Protection Portfolio.

Medicare

Medicare is the largest federal health insurance program, and it is the major health insurer for Americans over the age of 65 and Americans who are disabled. Once you qualify, you can use Original Medicare, which is a traditional fee-for-service health plan, or, in many cases, you can use a managed care organization that contracts with Medicare. If you are 65 or older, you can get a certain amount of coverage for hospital and physician visits from Medicare.

The type of coverage Medicare offers depends on whether you are covered by Medicare Part A, Part B, or both:

• **Medicare, Part A:** If you qualify for Social Security you are automatically covered by Medicare Part A. In most cases there is no premium charge to you for this coverage. Part A typically covers inpatient-type benefits such as hospital care, skilled nursing facility, home health care, and hospice care.

• **Medicare, Part B:** Part B coverage is not automatic. It is voluntary coverage for which you must apply at the age of 65 or later and for which a monthly premium (in 2003, the premium is $58.70 a month) will be charged. This premium is commonly deducted from your Social Security check. When you become eligible for Part A benefits, you will be sent an enrollment form for Part B, but you should fill it out only if you want to reject the coverage. If you fail to reject coverage within two months from the date you receive the form, you will automatically be enrolled in Part B. If you opt out, you can enroll later, but at a higher cost to you. Part B provides for physician's services, outpatient hospital care, physical therapy, the use of medical equipment, and ambulance expenses. Note: Neither of these policies provides coverage for dental care, vision care, or, as of this writing, prescription drugs. Also, Medicare has very limited coverage for long-term care.

When you sign up for Medicare, you'll receive a card and a pamphlet describing your benefits under the program. Please keep both in your Protection Portfolio for future reference. If you lose your Medicare card, you can obtain a replacement card from the Social Security Administration by calling 800-772-1213 or logging on to *www.ssa.gov.* You will need to supply the following information:

❑ Name as it appears on your most recent Social Security card
❑ Social Security number
❑ Date and place of birth
❑ Mother's maiden name
❑ Phone number
❑ Amount of last payment or the month and year you last received a payment if you have received benefits in the last 12 months.

Medigap Insurance

Since Medicare will not cover all your medical costs and since it also requires that you pay deductibles in order to receive benefits, you may want to buy additional coverage. Medigap policies have been designed by private insurers to supplement Medicare coverage (although not to cover long-term care). There are many types of Medigap policies, and they vary in quality and cost. Look for a policy that covers at least a 20-percent coinsurance cost for doctors' bills, hospital and doctor-visit deductibles, preventive care, and excess doctor fees. Don't buy more than one of these policies, because you will be paying twice for some benefits. Keep your policy and plan description in your Protection Portfolio.

Managed Care Organizations

A managed care organization (MCO) works like an HMO, as follows: The organization you select becomes the recipient of the premium that you pay out of your Social Security check. In exchange for that fixed monthly payment from Medicare, the provider takes care of your medical needs. Some HMOs and MCOs do not charge anything beyond the Medicare premiums; some charge more but offer additional services that may eliminate the need for Medigap insurance. Getting coverage via an MCO or HMO is, in my opinion, the preferred way to go because, in general, you can be adequately covered at a far lower cost than through Medigap. Again, please keep your policy and plan description in your Protection Portfolio.

Medicaid

Medicaid (called MediCal in California) is a combined federal and state welfare program that covers medical care for poor Americans. In order to qualify, you must be poor or medically needy, over age 65 or under age 21, blind, disabled, or receiving certain welfare benefits. Keep a copy of your card in your Protection Portfolio. For a list of toll-free state phone numbers to contact Medicaid, log onto *www.hcfa.gov/medicaid/obs5.htm.*

Long-Term-Care Insurance

As many of you know, I am a huge proponent of long-term-care insurance, which can protect your assets and your loved ones' financial security in case you suffer a catastrophic or chronic illness that requires extended home care or a nursing home stay. Given that one out of three of us will spend time in a nursing home after age 65, long-term-care insurance is

used more than any other kind of insurance.

Your health insurance will not pay for long-term care, and in most cases Medicare won't, either. Medicaid will, but only if you are destitute. If you are in your mid-to-late 50s or older and can afford long-term-care insurance, I urge you to look into it. It is an important step to take today to make sure that your loved ones' tomorrows are financially protected.

If you own a long-term-care policy, please keep your policy in your Protection Portfolio.

Long-Term Disability Insurance

Long-term-disability (LTD) insurance can protect you if a catastrophe prevents your being able to work and earn a living. LTD will usually pay 60 to 70 percent of your current salary in the event of a disability due to illness, accident, or another kind of disaster.

Finding good LTD insurance can be complicated and expensive, but if your paycheck—or your life partner's paycheck—is important to your family's security, it is well worth looking into. When shopping for LTD, one thing to consider is whether the policy will pay in case of being unable to perform the "owner's occupation" or "any occupation." Will the insurance company pay you only if your accident or illness leaves you unable to perform any job whatsoever, or will it pay if you cannot perform your job? Needless to say, the policy you want is the one that will provide benefits if you are unable to perform the job you are trained for. Most policies pay only until you are 65 years of age and thus eligible for retirement benefits.

If you own a long-term-disability policy, please keep it in your Protection Portfolio.

Social Security Statements & Cards

Chapter Seven

SOCIAL SECURITY STATEMENTS & CARDS

Please locate and collect the documents listed in the "Social Security Documents Checklist" at right and file each document in your Protection Portfolio. If you cannot find a document, go to the Protection Portfolio Forms CD-ROM and find links to Websites from which you can download forms for a replacement Social Security card or request a copy of your annual Social Security statement. Once a listed document has been located and filed, check it off on the printed checklist on your file folder.

Planning with Social Security

When planning for your retirement, don't forget to take into account your Social Security benefits. Each year, about three months before your birthday, you should receive by mail an updated estimate of the monthly amount of Social Security benefits you can expect to receive at retirement. If you haven't received such an estimate, please request a Social Security statement by submitting the form **"Social Security Statement Request."** On your Protection Portfolio Forms CD-ROM, you will find a link to access this form at:

www.ssa.gov/online/ssa-7004.html

Your Social Security Statement

This is a record of your earning history and an estimate of how much you and your employer(s) have paid in Social Security taxes; and an estimate of the benefits you (and your family) may be eligible for now and in the future. The benefit estimates in your Social Security statement can play an important role in your financial planning. When combined with your savings, investments, voluntary retirement programs, and pensions, your Social Security benefits can help

> ### SOCIAL SECURITY DOCUMENTS CHECKLIST
>
> ❑ Annual Social Security statement
> ❑ Social Security card
> ❑ Photocopies of spouse's or life partner's and children's Social Security cards
> ❑ Copies of checks of paid self-insurance tax

create a secure future for you and your loved ones. But mistakes could keep you from receiving all the benefits you deserve. Every year, check your statement to make sure that the record of your wages and other information (even such basics as your name and date of birth) are correct and up to date. The sooner you identify mistakes, the easier it is to correct them. Once you're sure your statement is correct, file it in your Protection Portfolio.

Please note: Your Social Security statement reflects only your earning and tax history. It doesn't contain information about any benefits you might qualify for under a spouse's or someone else's record. To ask about that, call 800-772-1213 or visit a local Social Security office (listed in the blue pages of your phone book).

How to Get a New or a Replacement Social Security Card

If you've never had a Social Security card, or if you need a replacement card or have legally changed your name and need a card under your new name, you have to submit the form **"Application for a Social Security Card"** to the Social Security Administration. On your Protection Portfolio Forms CD-ROM, you will find a link to access this form at:

www.ssa.gov/online/ss-5.html

When you've printed the form, completed it, and are ready to mail or bring it to your Social Security office, you will need to include documents that prove your identity.

These must be either originals or copies certified by the agency issuing the documents. (If you mail your application, your proofs of identity will be returned to you when you receive your card.)

Documents that Social Security accepts as proofs of identity are: a passport, a driver's license, a marriage or divorce certificate, military record of service, an adoption certificate, an employer ID card, a life insurance policy, a health insurance card (not a Medicare card), and a school ID card. For instructions on how to obtain copies of many of these personal documents, see the section on "Personal Documents." Please note: If you are requesting a name change, you'll need to mail or bring one or more documents identifying you by both your old name and your new name.

Once you apply with all the necessary documentation, you can expect to receive your card within about two weeks.

Your Social Security Benefits

Full Social Security retirement benefits have traditionally been payable at age 65 (with reduced benefits available as early as age 62) to anyone with enough Social Security credits, which are based on your earnings over time. This has changed; now, the age at which full benefits are paid depends on the year in which you were born, and that age will rise in future years. For example, if you were born in or before 1937, Social Security considers your full retirement age to be the traditional age of 65. But if you were born in 1960, Social Security considers your full retirement age to be 67. Just as people who retire early receive decreased benefits, people who delay their retirement beyond their official retirement age receive increased benefits when they retire.

In most cases, no matter what age you decide to start collecting, your payments will begin the month after your birthday. Social Security automatically adjusts for inflation on January 1 every year, based on the rise or fall in the previous year's consumer price

Retirement Ages Based on Year of Birth and Percentages of Benefits

If you were born in	You turned 62 in	Benefits at 62	Full retirement benefits at
1937 or before	1999 or before	80%	65
1938	2000	79.2%	65, 2 mo
1939	2001	78.3%	65, 4 mo
1940	2002	77.5%	65, 6 mo
1941	2003	76.7%	65, 8 mo
1942	2004	75.8%	65, 10 mo
1943-54	2005-2016	75%	66
1955	2017	75.2%	66, 2 mo
1956	2018	73.3%	66, 4 mo
1957	2019	72.5%	66, 6 mo
1958	2020	71 .7%	66, 8 mo
1959	2021	70.8%	66, 10 mo
1960 or later	2022	70%	67

index (an index of prices for everyday goods and services). Since the cost of living rarely goes down, count on a yearly increase in benefits of up to 3 percent.

Traditionally, you have been able to claim benefits at age 62 and receive a 20 percent reduction in benefits. Now there is a sliding scale. Consult the table on the previous page to find out where you stand.

Why Collecting Social Security at Age 62 May Make More Sense for You

In my opinion—unless you want to continue to work after retirement—the majority of you should probably consider taking Social Security benefits when you are 62 rather than waiting until you are 65. Here's why.

Let's say that at age 65 you would be entitled to receive $1,000 a month, while at age 62 you would be entitled to receive only $800 a month. Believe it or not, you could be losing money if you waited. If you took your benefits early, then during those 36 months, from age 62 to age 65, you would be receiving $800 a month that you wouldn't otherwise get, for a total of $28,800 ($800 x 36). If you waited until age 65 to collect the $1,000 a month, you would get $200 more a month, but the question is: beginning at age 65, how long would it take you to save $28,800 if you put away your extra $200 a month? The answer is 12 years (not including any interest that your money might earn). By taking Social Security at 62, you have received this money in three years, not 12.

Another way to look at it is to imagine that you take the $800 a month and save it. In three years you would have approximately $30,000, including interest. If you invested this money at a 6 percent interest rate, you would receive an income of $150 a month. This, added to your monthly Social Security payment of $800, would give you $950—only $50 less than the $1,000 you

would receive from Social Security if you waited until age 65. The difference, of course, is that although you might be receiving $50 less a month, you would have $30,000 in the bank. If interest rates climbed to 10 percent, your income on the $30,000 would also increase—to $250 a month, giving you a total income of $1,050 a month. Of course, if interest rates fell—say, to 3 percent a year—your income would fall, too—to $75 a month, giving you a total income of only $875. In most cases, the option of taking your Social Security at age 62 is worth looking into.

Working After Social Security Begins

If you are younger than age 65 and collecting Social Security benefits, you may be penalized for continuing to work, but less so than in the past. If you are 65 or older, as of the year 2000 you can earn as much as you like and not have your benefits reduced.

The new formula for reducing the benefits of Social Security recipients who are 62 to 64 and continue to work is as follows:

If you are under the current full retirement age of 65 when you start getting your Social Security payments, $1 in benefits will be deducted for each $2 you earn above the annual limit. For 2003, that limit is $11,520.

As of 2003, in the year you reach full retirement age, $1 in benefits will be deducted for each $3 you earn above a $30,720 limit, but only counting earnings before the month you reach the full benefit retirement age.

Starting the month you reach full retirement age, you will get your benefits with no limit on your earnings.

Survivor and Divorce Benefits

If you are not already receiving Social Security benefits when a spouse or an ex-spouse dies, you should apply for survivor benefits immediately. You can apply either over the phone or in person at your local Social Security office. The amount of your benefit will be based on the earnings of the person who died and how much he or she paid into Social Security. Your benefit amount is a percentage of the deceased worker's basic Social Security benefit. Here are some typical scenarios:

• *You are widowed.* Many widows and widowers receive their deceased spouse's Social Security benefits. But you must be 60 to apply (50 if you are disabled). You must be unmarried at the time you apply. Otherwise, you will not be eligible for survivor benefits.

Generally, you can't receive survivor's benefits if you remarry. But there are exceptions. If you are age 60 or older (50, if disabled) and have already begun to receive benefits, you can remarry and continue to receive them. Once you turn 62, you can choose to receive benefits on the record of your new spouse instead, if those are higher.

• *You are widowed and divorced.* If you are divorced from your spouse and he or she dies, you will be entitled to survivor benefits if you were married to him or her for at least ten years. The rules for applying for benefits are the same as above, except for the length of the marriage.

• *You are widowed and your spouse was not yet age 62.* Depending on your age and whether or not you have children, you may be eligible for a percentage of your deceased spouse's benefits. What percentage will depend on how old you are (not how old your spouse was) and the type of benefit you are eligible for. The following are typical:

- Widow or widower, age 65 or older: 100%
- Widow or widower age, 60-64: about 71-94%
- Widow, any age, with a child under age 16: 75%
- Children: 75%

In most cases, survivor benefits will not be retroactive. To process your application, Social Security may need the following original documents or certified copies: a birth certificate for you; a death certificate for your deceased spouse; Social Security numbers for your deceased spouse, you, and any dependent children; a marriage certificate; divorce papers (if you're a surviving an ex-spouse); your deceased spouse's W-2 forms or federal self-employment tax returns for the most recent year; the name of your bank and your account number, so benefits can be directly deposited into your account.

• *You are divorced and your spouse is alive.* If you are divorced from your spouse and he or she is still alive, to collect benefits you must be 62 years old when you apply, have been married to your ex-spouse for at least ten years, and be unmarried at the time you apply. Should you remarry after receiving benefits, you will not be entitled to further benefits from the first spouse. If you divorce again, you can return to receiving benefits from the first spouse, if these benefits are higher, or from the second spouse if you meet the application requirements above.

Dependents Benefits If the Disability Beneficiary Dies

When someone in your family who has been receiving disability benefits dies, payments to the family members will become survivors' benefits. In order for Social Security to change disability benefits over to survivor benefits, it needs you to mail or deliver a certified copy of the deceased's death certificate or another proof of death.

While you're waiting for this to happen, be careful not to cash any new disability check made out to the deceased. Instead, return it to Social Security. (No payment is due for the month of the death.) If the deceased was using direct deposit, the bank should be notified. If the payment is issued jointly, the survivor must contact his or her local Social Security office.

Your Retirement Plans

Chapter Eight

YOUR RETIREMENT PLANS

Please locate the documents listed in the "Retirement Plan Documents Checklist" at right and file them in your Protection Portfolio. Once a document has been filed, check it off on the printed checklist on your file folder.

When the time comes for you to begin withdrawing money from your retirement accounts, please store records of those transactions in the Protection Portfolio for at least three years.

Time and Your Retirement Plans

Retirement planning is a linchpin of financial security for you and your family. After all, each of us will one day have to live on the money we have saved rather than the money we are earning. The time to start planning for that day is now. Please answer yes or no to the following questions:

	YES	NO
If you are employed by a company or firm that offers a retirement plan, are you currently participating in it (or planning to participate when you are eligible)?	❑	❑
If you are self-employed, do your contribute to a Keogh plan or SEP-IRA?	❑	❑
In either case, are you making the maximum contribution allowed by law?	❑	❑

If you did not answer yes to both questions, I have to tell you that, in my opinion, you are making one of the biggest financial mistakes possible, next to getting into serious credit card debt.

RETIREMENT PLAN DOCUMENTS CHECKLIST

❑ Pension plan summary description, annual plan statement, and annual individual pension benefit statement
❑ Money-purchase/profit-sharing plan documents
❑ Beneficiary designations
❑ Retirement account withdrawals

How Will You Pay Your Bills When You're Retired?

Let me ask you one more question: If you cannot afford to put money away for your retirement because you do not have enough money to pay your bills now, while you have a paycheck coming in, how do you expect to pay exactly the same bills when you no longer have a paycheck? Write your answers below.

_____

_____

_____

There is no answer, because you will not be able to pay your bills. The solution: If you start now, you can put aside an impressive amount of money—even on a modest salary. So once again, I urge you to start saving today for your tomorrows.

How to Save More—and More Wisely—for Retirement

• *If you do not have credit card debt*, and if you are signed up at work for a 401(k), 403(b), 457, or SIMPLE plan, I want you to go to your human resources department and increase your contribution to the maximum amount allowable. If you have not signed up for your retirement plan, please do so now. If you are self-employed or your place of employment doesn't offer a 401(k) or a similar plan, please read on and take the actions that are right for you.

• *If you do have credit card debt,* and if you are eligible to invest in your 401(k), 403(b), 457, or SIMPLE plan, please answer yes or no to the following questions:

	YES	NO
Is the interest rate on your credit card debt higher than the average rate of return on your 401(k) or similar retirement plan?	❏	❏
Do you hate having credit card debt ?	❏	❏

If you answered yes to both questions, I want you to begin changing the way you contribute to your 401(k) or similar retirement plan, based on whether or not your company matches your contribution. Please consult the chart below.

Employer-Sponsored Retirement Plans: How They Work to Protect You

The plans known as 401(k), 403(b), 457, and SIMPLE all allow you to contribute a percentage of your salary on a tax-deferred basis to a retirement savings program, to which your employer may or may not contribute a full or partial matching amount. A 401(k), which takes its exciting

If You Have Credit Card Debt — How to Contribute to Your 401(k) or Similar Retirement Plan		
If the company does not match your contribution and the interest rate on your credit card is higher than the return on your 401(k) or similar retirement plan.	**If the company does match your contribution and the interest rate on your credit card is higher than the return on your 401(k) or similar retirement plan.**	**If the company does match your contribution and the interest rate on your credit card is lower than the return on your 401(k) or similar retirement plan.**
You should stop contributing to your 401(k) or similar plan and take every dollar you would have been contributing to the plan and put it toward paying off your credit card debt. After your debt is paid in full, go back to contributing to your 401(k) or similar plan.	You should contribute to your 401(k) or similar plan to up to the point of the match. After you have reached the maximum amount of money that your company will match, stop contributing and take that money and put it toward paying off the debt.	If you do not mind having credit card debt and you are 40 years of age or younger, continue to invest fully in your 401(k) plan— or least to the level of the match. At the same time, continue to pay off your credit card debt.

name from a section of the tax code, is an all-around plan that almost any company can enter into. A 403(b) plan is the plan you probably have if you work for a non-profit organization, such as a hospital, a university, or a research organization. A 457 plan is typically offered by state and local governments, but may also be offered by tax- exempt organizations; its rules can differ depending on whether a public or private employer sponsors it. (In the chart below, we deal only with government-sponsored 457 plans.) "SIMPLE" stands for Savings Incentive Match plan for Employees. It can be offered by companies that employ 100 or fewer people (each with at least $5,000 in compensation in the previous year) and that do not maintain another plan.

On the next page is a quick reference guide to employer-sponsored retirement plans.

Individual Retirement Accounts (IRAs)

In addition to contributing to an employer's retirement plan, you can also have a traditional individual retirement account (IRA). If you are covered by an employer's plan, however, whether you can defer taxes on your contributions will depend on your income. (For those of you who are not covered by an employer's plan, you can defer taxes on your contributions no matter what your income.)

Here are the income limits for deferring taxes on your contributions to a traditional IRA if you or a spouse are covered by an employer's plan.

For single people who are covered by an employer's retirement plan, the deductibility phases out between $34,000 and $44,000 in 2002, $40,000 and $50,000 in 2003, $45,000 and $55,000 in 2004, and $50,000 and $60,000 in 2005 and later.

For married people who are covered by an employer's plan, the deductibility phases out between $54,000 and $64,000 in 2002, $60,000 and $70,000 in 2003, $65,000 and $75,000 in 2004, $70,000 and $80,000 in 2005, $75,000 and $85,000 in 2006, and $80,000 and $100,000 in 2007 and later.

For married people who are not covered by an employer's plan but have a spouse who is covered by an employer's plan, the deductibility phases out between $150,000 and $160,000.

Under any circumstances, the maximum amount you can contribute to an IRA for the years 2002–2004 is $3,000 if you are under age 50, or $3,500 if you are 50 or older.

Consider a Roth IRA

Besides having a traditional IRA, you can also contribute to a Roth IRA if you meet certain income qualifications. Single taxpayers whose modified adjusted gross income (MAGI) is less than $95,000 per year, and married couples filing a joint return who have a combined annual MAGI of less than $150,000 for 2002–2004, can contribute up to $3,000 each if they are under 50, or $3,500 if they are over 50. Your eligibility to contribute the full $3,000 (or $3,500 if you are over 50) is phased out between an income of $95,000 and $110,000 for single taxpayers and between $150,000 and $160,000 for married taxpayers filing jointly. After those income amounts, you are not eligible for a Roth IRA.

With a Roth IRA, contributions are not tax deductible, but your contributions can grow tax-free rather than tax deferred. That means that when you withdraw money from a Roth IRA at retirement, you will not owe any taxes on any of the money you withdraw, no matter how much the money has grown in value (provided you have followed IRS guidelines). In addition, with a Roth

Quick Reference Guide: Employer-Sponsored Retirement Plans

	401(k)/403(b)	Governmental 457	SIMPLE
Definition	A voluntary retirement plan offered to employees of companies. Plans allow up to a certain percentage of employees' pretax pay to be set aside and invested within the retirement plan.	A voluntary retirement plan, typically offered to employees of state, county, and city governments, that allows up to a certain percentage of employees' pretax pay to be set aside and invested within the retirement plan. Please note: 457 plans may also be offered to employees of tax-exempt or non-profit organizations, but provisions may differ from those listed here.	A voluntary retirement plan (Savings Incentive Match for Employees) set up by small businesses for their employees. Employees receive some level of matching contribution from employer.
What is the maximum contribution?	Year Under 50 Over 50 2002 $11,000 $12,000 2003 $12,000 $14,000 2004 $13,000 $16,000 2005 $14,000 $18,000 2006 $15,000 $20,000 After 2006, increases will be indexed in $500 increments based upon inflation.	Year Under 50 Over 50 2002 $11,000 $12,000 2003 $12,000 $14,000 2004 $13,000 $16,000 2005 $14,000 $18,000 2006 $15,000 $20,000 After 2006, increases will be indexed in $500 increments based upon inflation. Please note: In government 457 plans, as of 2002 a special catch-up rule applies if you are three or fewer years away from retirement, letting you contribute up to twice the annual maximum amount in any given year.	Year Under 50 Over 50 2002 $7,000 $7,500 2003 $8,000 $9,000 2004 $9,000 $10,500 2005 $10,000 $12,000 2006 $12,500 After 2005 for those under 50 and after 2006 for those over 50, increases will be indexed in $500 increments based upon inflation.
When and how am I taxed?	Taxes are deferred until you take your money out, at which time it will be taxed as ordinary income.	Taxes are deferred until you take your money out, at which time it will be taxed as ordinary income.	Taxes are deferred until you take your money out, at which time it will be taxed as ordinary income.
When can I withdraw funds?	In most cases you cannot withdraw the funds prior to age 59½ without paying a 10% federal penalty, as well as a state income tax penalty, on the amount withdrawn.	Funds can be withdrawn when you retire from or leave your employer's service. A government-sponsored 457 plan is different from a 401(k) or a 403(b) plan in that there is no mandatory minimum retirement age and no 10% federal penalty for early withdrawal of funds. As of 2002, under certain conditions, rollover of assets from government-sponsored 457 plans into other retirement plans, such as IRAs, 401(k)s, 403(b)s and other 457 plans, is allowed.	In most cases you cannot withdraw the funds prior to age 59½ without paying a 10% federal penalty, as well as a state income tax penalty, on the amount withdrawn. In addition, if you take out funds during the first two years you participate in the plan, an early withdrawal tax of 25% will apply.

IRA, you do not have to wait until you are $59\frac{1}{2}$ to begin taking withdrawals, as you do with a traditional IRA; you can take out your original contributions at any time, for any purpose, regardless of your age, without incurring taxes or penalties. Any earnings on your contributions, however, must remain in the Roth IRA until you turn $59\frac{1}{2}$ and have held the account for more than five years; otherwise, you will incur taxes and penalties on the earnings amounts you withdraw. Earnings from a Roth IRA can, however, be withdrawn penalty-free if you become disabled or die.

Please note: You can have both a traditional IRA and a Roth IRA, but you can contribute only the maximum total amount allowed (in 2003, $3,000, or $3,500 for those 50 or older) each year to all your lRAs, no matter how many you have or what kind they are.

See the chart on the next page for a comparison of traditional lRAs and Roth lRAs.

Retirement Plans for the Self-Employed

If you are self-employed, you also have excellent retirement-planning options, in addition to funding a traditional or a Roth IRA. These include opening a SEP-IRA or a Keogh plan, either of which offers a great way to save for retirement. If you qualify, as of 2002 you may be able to save up to 25 percent of your income or a maximum dollar amount of $40,000, whichever is less. To qualify for these retirement programs, you must report your earnings on Form 1099-MISC or earn income as fees for services you've provided. If you have people working for you and open and SEP-IRA or Keogh for yourself, after a certain period of time you'll have to fund one for them as well. If you are thinking of setting up an SEP-IRA or a Keogh, it's best to consult an accountant familiar with these plans.

Traditional Pension Plans

You've worked all your life to be able to retire. Now, when you reach retirement age, if you are going to receive a basic pension from your company (not a 401(k) or other voluntary plan), then you are going to have to make a choice about how to take that pension so that it will preserve and protect the income you may need to live on for the rest of your life. You may not have to make the decision right away; many companies will allow you to keep your pension money in the company plan for at least one year after your retirement date, and most will allow you to keep it there indefinitely. Until you know exactly what you are going to want to do with your money, don't rush into anything! Protect yourself by taking time to weigh your options and plan your strategies carefully.

Should You Take a Monthly Pension or a Lump-Sum Payment?

Whether it's best for you to receive your pension money in a lump-sum payment or as a monthly pension check depends on the following factors:

- How much you have in your pension account
- The amount of the monthly payment the company will give you
- The amount of the monthly payment the company will pay to your spouse or life partner after you have died
- Your age
- Your life expectancy and the life expectancy of your spouse
- Whether you need this income to live on
- Whether this income needs to support another person after you have died

To decide between taking your pension as a lump sum or as monthly payments, start by looking at the actual return you would get if you took the monthly pension payments. Then compare that to what you could reasonably expect to get on your own if you took a lump sum and invested it.

IRA Comparisons			
	Traditional IRA	**Spousal IRA**	**Roth IRA**
Tax Deferred?	Yes (in most cases)	Yes (in most cases)	No
Taxable at withdrawal?	Yes	Yes	No (if you meet qualifications)
10% Penalty for premature withdrawal?	Yes, prior to 59½	Yes, prior to 59½	Yes, for earnings withdrawn prior to age 59½ and earlier than five years from when the Roth was funded. Original contributions can be withdrawn tax- and penalty-free at any time.
Mandatory withdrawal age?	70	70	No
Penalty-free withdrawals?	$10,000 for first-time home buyers, or unlimited for educational purposes.	$10,000 for first-time home buyers, or unlimited for educational purposes.	$10,000 for first-time home buyers, or unlimited for educational purposes.
Maximum contribution?	Year Under 50 Over 50 2002 $3,000 $3,500 2003 $3,000 $3,500 2004 $3,000 $3,500 2005 $4,000 $4,500 2006 $4,000 $5,000 2007 $4,000 $5,000 2008 $5,000 $6,000 After 2008, increases will be indexed in $500 increments based upon inflation.	Year Under 50 Over 50 2002 $3,000 $3,500 2003 $3,000 $3,500 2004 $3,000 $3,500 2005 $4,000 $4,500 2006 $4,000 $5,000 2007 $4,000 $5,000 2008 $5,000 $6,000 After 2008, increases will be indexed in $500 increments based upon inflation.	Year Under 50 Over 50 2002 $3,000 $3,500 2003 $3,000 $3,500 2004 $3,000 $3,500 2005 $4,000 $4,500 2006 $4,000 $5,000 2007 $4,000 $5,000 2008 $5,000 $6,000 After 2008, increases will be indexed in $500 increments based upon inflation.

Monthly Pension Versus Lump-Sum Payment Worksheet

Please go to the Protection Portfolio Forms CD-ROM and print out the **"Monthly Pension Versus Lump-Sum Payment"** worksheet, which you may need to use as we proceed.

Let's say that you are 60 years old and are being offered a choice between a $250,000 lump sum or $1,300 a month for the rest of your life. There's a joint and survivor benefit attached (please see page 66), so when you die, your life partner or spouse would receive half of the monthly pension amount ($650 a month).

To figure out the rate of return on your monthly pension amount, we need to do some math.

1. Take the monthly pension amount that your company is offering you and multiply it by 12. This is how much you will receive in pension payments every year.

Example monthly pension	**You** monthly pension
$1,300	$
x12	x12
$15,600	$
annual pension payments	annual pension payments

2. Take the amount of your annual pension payments and divide it by the lump sum you are being offered. This answer is, in essence, the percentage return the company is giving you on your money.

Example annual pension	**You** annual pension
$ 15,600	$
÷lump sum $250,000	÷lump sum $
percentage return .0624 or 6.24%	percentage return

3. Do these calculations again, this time using the amount that your surviving spouse or life partner will get. To do this, take the monthly pension amount that your company is offering your surviving spouse or life partner and multiply it by 12. This is how much he or she will receive in pension payments every year.

Example spouse monthly pension	**Your spouse** monthly pension
$ 650	$
x12	x12
$7,800	$
annual pension payments	annual pension payments

4. Take the amount of your surviving spouse's or life partner's annual pension payments and divide it by the lump sum your surviving spouse or life partner is being offered. This answer is, in essence, the percentage return the company is giving you on your money when it comes to paying your surviving spouse or life partner.

Example annual pension	**You** annual pension
$ 7,800	$
÷lump sum $250,000	÷lump sum $
percentage return .0312 or 3.12%	percentage return

5. Substituting your numbers for the numbers in the worksheet example above, ask yourself this question:

Do you think that over your life expectancy you can earn 6.24 percent a year on your money without risk and that after you die your spouse or life partner could earn 3.12 percent?

YES ❑   NO ❑

6. Using your actual numbers from the worksheet you completed above, fill in the blanks:

> Do you think that over your life expectancy you can earn _____ percent a year on your money without risk and that after you die your spouse or life partner could earn _____ percent?
>
> YES ❑   NO ❑

If your answer is no, you couldn't possibly earn the rate of return that the company is offering to provide, then you might be best off taking the monthly pension option. But if the numbers are close, and they probably will be, then it will pay you to look at other investment options, keeping in mind that, if you do take the monthly pension option, you will no longer have the principal available for you or your beneficiaries. If you decide to look into other investment options, please consult a fee-based investment adviser who has been working as an adviser for at least 10 to 15 years.

Joint and Survivor Pension Benefits

If you are going to receive a basic pension when you retire, you usually have the option of reducing your monthly pension amount in exchange for the promise that your spouse or life partner will continue to receive some portion of your monthly pension amount after you die. This is called a joint and survivor option. You can often choose among several levels of joint and survivor benefits, usually 100 percent, 75 percent, 50 percent, and 25 percent. The larger the percentage of your monthly pension you want your spouse or life partner to get, the more money will be deducted from your basic pension payment each month while you live. (Federal law requires written permission from your spouse if you opt to take less than a 50 percent joint and survivor benefit on a tax-qualified pension plan. Some states make the same requirement in the case of non-company plans, such as IRAs.)

Not all companies make it financially affordable to take a joint and survivor option. Each company has its own pricing structure, so you must first figure out how much each option will cost. The following will help guide you through this decision-making process if you are about to retire. If you are still years away from retirement, your company may be able to do a projection so you can get an idea of what your joint and survivor benefits will be.

Which Joint and Survivor Benefit Option Might Be Best for You?

Please go to the Protection Portfolio Forms CD-ROM and print out the "Which Joint and Survivor Benefit Option Might Be Best for You?" worksheet, which you may need to use as we proceed.

Fill in the blanks from the information on your benefit sheet and follow the instructions on the next pages.

Joint/Survivor Benefit Options				
Item	J&S Options	Employee	Partner Benefit	Cost
1.	Basic pension	(A) ____	(B) ____	(C) ____
2.	50% option	(D) ____	(E) ____	(F) ____
3.	100% option	(G) ____	(H) ____	(I) ____

Item 1

• In (A), write the amount of your basic pension. This is how much the company will give you monthly. Upon your death, your partner gets nothing.
• In (B), place a "0." This is how much your partner will receive from your pension benefits if you pass away first.
• In (C), place a "0." When you take this option, there is no cost to you because there is no survivor benefit to pay for. The company

owes you the basic pension, and this is what it will pay you.

Item 2
• In (D), write the dollar amount that appears in the "50 percent joint and survivor" section of your benefit statement.
• In (E), take (D) and divide by 2. This is what your partner will receive after your death. This figure should also appear on your benefit statement.
• In (F), subtract (D) from (A) and enter that sum here. This is the cost to you for the 50 percent option.

Item 3
• In (G), write the dollar amount that appears in the "100 percent joint and survivor" section on your benefit statement.
• In (H), write the same figure that appears in (G). This is the benefit your surviving partner will receive. You should also find this figure on your benefit statement.
• In (I), subtract (G) from (A) and write this figure here. This is the cost to you for the 100 percent J&S option.

The Case of Don and Janet
Once you have filled in the blanks, you will have something that looks like the example below, which examines the pension choices of a hypothetical couple we'll call Don and Janet. Don is 56 and Janet is 54. Don is about to take early retirement.

	Joint/Survivor Benefit Options			
Item	**J&S Options**	**Don**	**Janet**	**Cost**
1.	Basic pension	(A) $2,090	(B) $0	(C) $0
2.	50% option	(D) $2,000	(E) $1,000	(F) $90
3.	100% option	(G) $1,843	(H) $1,843	(I) $247

Explanation
In Item 1, Don's basic pension is $2,090 a month. If Don and Janet choose this option, Janet will receive absolutely no monthly income upon Don's death.

If Don and Janet take the 50 percent joint and survivor benefit option in Item 2, the $2,090 is reduced to $2,000 during Don's lifetime, and Janet will receive $1,000 a month if and when Don dies. The cost to them for this option is $90 a month.

In Item 3, taking the 100 percent J&S option reduces the monthly income Don and Janet get while Don is alive from $2,090 to $1,843 in order to provide Janet with $1,843 a month for the rest of her life upon Don's death. The cost to them for this option is $247 a month.

Now that Don and Janet know what the cost to them will be for each J&S option, they need to decide which option they will take. Don and Janet decide that they want to take the 100 percent joint and survivor benefit of $1,843 per month. This will cost them $247 a month, or $2,964 a year while Don lives.

When you and your life partner have to make a decision that will affect your financial future for the rest of your lives, please, please take time to consider your objectives and the ramifications of your choices. Once a joint and survivor option has been chosen, the choice is irreversible. All too often people think they should take more money now, without considering the future consequences. Please, please do the math. Do not tempt fate.

Your Pension Plan: Knowing Your Rights
By now, we've all heard stories about companies mismanaging their pension plans, leaving employees who have worked there for 20 years or more with nothing to retire on. If that makes you nervous, then the best thing you can do is to protect your future by keeping

track of what your company does with your retirement plan. Yes—you can do this.

The Employee Retirement Income Security Act of 1974 (ERISA) is a federal law that sets minimum standards for pension plans in private industry. ERISA requires retirement plan administrators—the people who run the plans—to provide you with written information explaining the most important facts about your pension plan. The plan administrator is required to keep you regularly informed. This includes a summary plan description (SPD), which you should get when you begin participating in the plan and which your should keep in the "Retirement" pocket of your Protection Portfolio.

The SPD is a comprehensive document that tells you exactly what the plan provides and how it operates. The SPD should show when you began to participate in the plan, how your service and benefits are calculated, when your benefit becomes vested, when and how you will receive payments, and how to file for your benefits when you need to. If there are any changes to the SPD, your plan administrator is required to give you a revised summary plan description or a separate document detailing the modifications. Please file those in your Protection Portfolio as well.

In addition to the SPD, the plan administrator must give you a copy of the plan's summary annual report, a summary of the yearly financial report that most pension plans must file with the Department of Labor. Finally, you should also receive, free of charge every year, an individual benefit statement that describes your personal total accrued and vested benefits. Please file these as well.

If the information you are given doesn't answer the questions you have about your plan, more information is available, but you must request it from the plan administrator.

Here are some facts you should know:

• *If you are vested in your pension, you have rights even if your lose your job.* If you leave an employer with whom you have a vested pension benefit that you won't be eligible to receive until later in life, your plan administrator must report that information to you and to the IRS, which, in turn, will inform the Social Security Administration. You can check with the Social Security Administration to ensure that you were reported as having a deferred vested benefit. Call the Social Security Administration toll-free at (800) 772-1213. Even if you don't request this information, Social Security will automatically fill you in when you retire and apply for Social Security benefits. Still, I think it is a good idea to double-check after you leave your job. Stay in touch with the plan administrator, keeping him or her informed of any name or address changes to ensure that you will receive your full pension benefit.

• *The law mandates that you start getting your pension benefits at a designated age and time.* According to the Employee Retirement Income Security Act, you must begin to receive plan payments from a qualified plan not later than the 60th day after the close of the plan year in which the last of the following events occurs:

1. You turn 65 (or the normal retirement age specified by your plan);

2. You have participated in your plan for at least 10 years; or

3. You terminate your service with the employer.

"Normal retirement age" is defined as the earlier of a) the age specified in the plan as normal retirement age; or b) age 65 or the fifth anniversary of the employee's participation in the plan, whichever is later.

Normal retirement age is also the point at which a participant must become 100 percent vested in the plan. So, for most people, being 100 percent vested in a qualified retirement plan is the factor that determines normal retirement age. These rules apply for both defined-contribution plans and defined-benefit plans.

• *Depending on the type of plan you have, you may be able to access benefits before the "normal retirement age."* Check your summary plan description for the specific details of your plan, but generally, there are several conditions under which your plan might allow you to begin receiving payments "early." A defined benefit plan could permit earlier payments by, say, providing for early retirement benefits, which might have additional eligibility requirements. A defined-benefit plan might also allow benefits to be paid out when you terminate your employment, suffer a disability, or die. Often, 401(k) plans allow you to withdraw some or all of your vested accrued benefit when you leave your job, reach age 59½, become disabled, retire, die, or suffer some other hardship that may be defined in the summary plan description. Profit-sharing or stock bonus plans may allow you to receive your vested accrued benefit after you leave your job, reach a specific age, become disabled, die, or after a specific number of years have elapsed.

• *If you are a part-time employee, you may be covered.* Employees who work at least 1,000 hours per year but do not work full-time must be credited with a pro rata portion of the benefit that they would accrue if they were employed full-time. In other words, if your plan requires that employees work at least 2,000 hours of service per year for full benefit accrual but you work only 1,000 hours per year, you will be credited with 50 percent of the full benefit. Check your summary plan description to see exactly how your plan calculates service credit.

• *Pension plans can be terminated, but any vested money you have in the plan may still be due you.* Pension plans are supposed to continue indefinitely, but employers are allowed to terminate plans. You do have some protection if your plan is canceled. If your plan is a qualified plan, your accrued benefit must become 100 percent vested when the plan terminates, to the extent that it is funded—meaning what has so far been contributed by you and your employer. This is also true if your employer partially terminates a qualified plan, for example, if one division of a company is closed and a substantial number of plan participants are affected. All affected employees' plans become 100 percent vested, to the extent they have been funded, effective as soon as the plan terminates.

• *Pension plans may be insured.* If you have a defined-benefit plan, ask your plan administrator if it is insured by the Pension Benefit Guaranty Corporation (PBGC). If it is, the PBGC guarantees that you will receive your vested pension benefits, up to certain limits. If additional benefits that exceed the PBGC's limits or that were not guaranteed are due to you, whether you receive them and how much you receive will depend on the plan's funding and how much the PBGC can recover from your employer. If you find yourself in this messy situation, contact the Pension Benefit Guaranty Corporation, Administrative Review and Technical Assistance Department, 1200 K Street NW, Washington, D.C. 20005, (202) 326-4000, for more information.

What to Keep in Your Protection Portfolio

Money-Purchase and Profit-Sharing Plan Documents

If you are self-employed or a small employer and have a money purchase retirement plan, a profit-sharing retirement plan, or a personal 401(k) that was set up for you or is administered by a pension administrator, please be sure to ask your administrator for the original or a copy of the plan agreement and keep it safe and sound in your Protection Portfolio.

Beneficiary Designations

IRAs, Keoghs, 401(k)s, 403(b)s, 457s, profit-sharing plans, and pensions are all types of retirement plans in which a custodian, usually a bank, a brokerage house, or your employer, retains the title to the account and you are the beneficiary. When you set up one of these accounts, part of the paperwork requires you to name a beneficiary or beneficiaries to receive the account when you die. The trouble is, many people forget who they designated as beneficiary when they created the account. In some cases, people get divorced, then die, without remembering to change the beneficiary designation, in which case the ex-spouse is legally entitled to receive the accounts. This is not what most people want. To be protected from this and other problems, please file copies of all the beneficiary designations you have made for all your retirement accounts in the Protection Portfolio. If you don't have a clue about these designations, contact the account holder or custodian and ask to receive a copy of the beneficiary designation on file for you. If you see that your beneficiaries are not who you want them to be, call the custodian and request a change of beneficiary form. Be sure to include not only a primary beneficiary but a contingent or secondary beneficiary, so if your first choice dies before you do (or with you), you get to control who gets the account. Don't name your estate as a beneficiary; this will require your family to probate the account.

If you want to make a donation to a charity at death, you can name the charity as a beneficiary on your account, or give a percentage of the account to the charity, and the charity will not pay a penny of income tax on the account. Any other beneficiary will be required to pay income tax on the tax-deferred dollars in the account, which is usually all of the account.

There are special rules for spouses, who may be able to roll the account over into their own name and not pay taxes until they withdraw the money. Such a decision may have a timeline that requires a decision to be made in writing and given to the custodian; otherwise, the spouse may lose the right to roll over the account.

Keep the copies of the designations in the protection portfolio until you change them, then file new copies.

Your Investments

Chapter Nine

YOUR INVESTMENTS

Please go to the Protection Portfolio Forms CD-ROM and print out the following worksheets, which you may need as we proceed:

- ❏ "Cash Accounts"
- ❏ " Mutual Funds, Money Market Accounts, Credit Unions"
- ❏ "Securities Accounts"
- ❏ "Partnerships, Limited Liability Companies, and Joint Ventures"
- ❏ "Individual Retirement Accounts (IRAs) or Pension Plans"

Please also locate the documents listed in the "Investment Documents Checklist" at right and file each one in your Protection Portfolio. Once a document has been filed, check it off on the printed checklist on your file folder.

For investment accounts, mutual funds, annuities, and other kinds of investments, you may receive statements monthly, quarterly, semi-annually, or every time you deposit more money into the investment vehicle. File these interim statements in your Protection Portfolio until the end of the year, then compare them to your annual statement and toss them, keeping only the year-end statement.

When you cash in an investment, store the record of that transaction in your Protection Portfolio for at least three years. Discard any records that are older than three years.

Protecting Your Investments

Although you may do much of your investing electronically—over the Internet or by phone—and many of your investments may be held by a broker or other financial institution, it is important to keep any original bonds, Treasury notes, stock certificates, bank certificates of deposit, or annuity contracts you may possess in a safe place. When the

INVESTMENT DOCUMENTS CHECKLIST

- ❏ Treasuries/Series I/Series EE/notes
- ❏ Stock certificates
- ❏ CDs
- ❏ Annuity contracts
- ❏ Stock option grant agreements
- ❏ Copies of all investment account application forms and agreements
- ❏ Investment documents asset list (forms located on pages 75–79 and on your Protection Portfolio CD-ROM)

time comes to cash these in, roll them over, or change them into something else, you will often have to produce the original. If you can't find the original, you will have to fill in an affidavit of lost originals, pay reissue fees, and do whatever else the company or agency that issued the documents wants you to do to authenticate your ownership. In some cases, the company or agency may not be able to find the proper documentation in its own records. In all cases, the process takes time.

Many people have personal corporations for their businesses. Often I have found that they forget to create or issue stock certificates for the corporation when they first set it up. If you have a personal corporation, you should have stock certificates that document who owns how many shares of the company. If you can't find these, then check with the lawyer who created the corporation. You should hold all your own original corporate documents, such as articles, bylaws, and minutes.

If you have created a limited liability company or limited partnership, the original agreements should be kept in the portfolio as well as any amendments to the member, operating, or partnership agreements.

It is also very helpful to have a list of assets that you own. You can use the forms provided on the following pages and on your Protection Portfolio Forms CD-ROM.

If you decide to keep some original documents in a safety deposit box, be sure to include the name of the bank, the bank address, the names of who has access to the box, and where the key is in your asset list. Then make copies of the documents that are in the safety deposit box, indicate the location of the original on the copy, and file these copies in the part of the Protection Portfolio where the originals would otherwise be kept.

Protecting Yourself in a Relationship with a Broker

If you do your investing through a brokerage firm and find that you've been given investment advice that's unsuitable for you because of your age, your financial situation, your investment objective, or your level of investing experience, you may be able to seek redress against your broker and the firm. Here are steps you may want to consider:

1. Write letters. Explain in writing why the advice you were given was unsuitable. Send a copy of your letter to the broker and to the firm's branch manager and compliance officer. Include a copy of your new account application or agreement, in which you or your broker indicated your level of risk tolerance and your investment goals. If the advice you received was in conflict with your stated level of risk tolerance or your stated goals, you may have a case against your broker and the firm.

2. File a complaint with the National Association of Securities Dealers and the Securities and Exchange Commission. Either or both of these agencies will investigate the broker and the firm to see whether there is a pattern of complaints like yours. You can file a complaint on-line by logging on to the National Association of Securities Dealers (NASD) Website at *www.nasdr.com* or to the Securities and Exchange Commission Website at *www.sec.gov.*

3. Contact a securities attorney. To find a securities attorney in your area, visit the Public Investors Arbitration Bar Association Website at *www.piaba.org.*

4. File an arbitration claim. For detailed information on how to start arbitration action, visit the NASD Website at *www.nasdr.com.*

Cash Accounts

For all cash accounts, please provide the information requested.

1. Name of Institution: _____

Branch & Address: _____

Type of Account and Account #: _____

Name(s) on Account: _____ Phone: _____

2. Name of Institution: _____

Branch & Address: _____

Type of Account and Account #: _____

Name(s) on Account: _____ Phone: _____

3. Name of Institution: _____

Branch & Address: _____

Type of Account and Account #: _____

Name(s) on Account: _____ Phone: _____

4. Name of Institution: _____

Branch & Address: _____

Type of Account and Account #: _____

Name(s) on Account: _____ Phone: _____

5. Name of Institution: _____

Branch & Address: _____

Type of Account and Account #: _____

Name(s) on Account: _____ Phone: _____

Mutual Funds, Money Market Accounts, Credit Unions

For all mutual funds you own, money market accounts you have, and credit unions you belong to, please provide the information requested. OR, you may attach a copy of the most recent monthly statement, which will contain all of the requested information.

1. Custodial Institution: _____

Address: _____

Name(s) on Account: _____   Phone: _____

Name of Fund: _____

Account #: _____

2. Custodial Institution: _____

Address: _____

Name(s) on Account: _____   Phone: _____

Name of Fund: _____

Account #: _____

3. Custodial Institution: _____

Address: _____

Name(s) on Account: _____   Phone: _____

Name of Fund: _____

Account #: _____

4. Custodial Institution: _____

Address: _____

Name(s) on Account: _____   Phone: _____

Name of Fund: _____

Account #: _____

Securities Accounts

For all securities accounts, please provide the information requested below. OR, you may attach a copy of a recent monthly statement, which will contain all of the requested information.

1. Name of Brokerage:

Brokerage Address:

Name(s) on Account:

Phone: Account #:

Your Account Representative:

2. Name of Brokerage:

Brokerage Address:

Name(s) on Account:

Phone: Account #:

Your Account Representative:

3. Name of Brokerage:

Brokerage Address:

Name(s) on Account:

Phone: Account #:

Your Account Representative:

4. Name of Brokerage:

Brokerage Address:

Name(s) on Account:

Phone: Account #:

Your Account Representative:

Partnerships, Limited Liability Companies, and Joint Ventures

For all partnerships in which you own an interest, please provide the information requested below.

Name of Partnership and General Partners: _____

Address: _____

Phone: _____

Name of Owner As It Appears on Partnership Records: _____

CIRCLE ONE: GENERAL PARTNER   LIMITED PARTNER   LLC

Amount of Original Investment: _____

Name of Partnership and General Partners: _____

Address: _____

Phone: _____

Name of Owner As It Appears on Partnership Records: _____

CIRCLE ONE: GENERAL PARTNER   LIMITED PARTNER   LLC

Amount of Original Investment: _____

Name of Partnership and General Partners: _____

Address: _____

Phone: _____

Name of Owner As It Appears on Partnership Records: _____

_____

CIRCLE ONE: GENERAL PARTNER   LIMITED PARTNER   LLC

Amount of Original Investment: _____

Individual Retirement Accounts (IRAs) or Pension Plans

For each Individual Retirement Account (IRA) and Pension Plan, such as a 401(k) profit-sharing plan, please provide the requested information. OR, you may attach a copy of the most recent annual statement, which will contain all of the requested information.

Participant's Name: _____

Account #: _____   CIRCLE ONE: IRA / or Pension Plan

Name and Address of Custodial Institution: _____

_____

Phone of Custodial Institution: _____

Name of Primary Beneficiary: _____

Name of Contingent Beneficiary: _____

Participant's Name: _____

Account #: _____   CIRCLE ONE: IRA / or Pension Plan

Name and Address of Custodial Institution: _____

_____

Phone of Custodial Institution: _____

Name of Primary Beneficiary: _____

Name of Contingent Beneficiary: _____

Participant's Name: _____

Account #: _____   CIRCLE ONE: IRA / or Pension Plan

Name and Address of Custodial Institution: _____

_____

Phone of Custodial Institution: _____

Name of Primary Beneficiary: _____

Name of Contingent Beneficiary: _____

Estate Planning Documents

Chapter Ten

ESTATE PLANNING

Please locate the documents listed in the "Estate Planning Documents Checklist" at right and file each of them in your Protection Portfolio. Once a document has been filed, check it off on the printed checklist on your file folder.

Many of you won't have the documents listed at right, and this section of the guidebook, along with the Protection Portfolio Forms CD-ROM, is intended to help you obtain and complete them. But even if you already have them, I strongly urge you to listen to the audio CDs we have supplied to make sure you have the correct documents in place and that you truly understand the uses and ramifications of the documents. Whenever you sign your name to any legal document, it is essential that you know what each clause means. This is the reason we created the audio CDs.

The Importance of the Advanced Directive and Power of Attorney for Health Care

As far as I'm concerned, the advanced directive and durable power of attorney for health care is the single most important document that you need to have in your portfolio. Most of the other documents that we'll be discussing are more beneficial for your heirs and for the people that you leave behind after you die. This one is for you.

For the sake of every one of you reading this guide, I hope that you won't ever be incapacitated or hospitalized, and that a long, healthy life awaits you. But just in case, I urge you to make the simple arrangements for an advanced directive and durable power of attorney for health care. Do this for yourself and for the people you love. Do it now, while you're strong and healthy. It might be the most important document you ever sign.

ESTATE PLANNING DOCUMENTS CHECKLIST

- ❑ Advanced Directive and Durable Power of Attorney for Health Care
- ❑ Financial Power of Attorney
- ❑ Will
- ❑ Will Affidavit
- ❑ Pour Over Will
- ❑ Revocable Living Trust
- ❑ Final Instructions
- ❑ Contracts of funeral or memorial arrangements
- ❑ Documentation of prepaid fees to cemetery and/or funeral home

The advanced directive and durable power of attorney for health care directly affects the quality of your life and the quality of your death—the manner in which you leave this world. The right to die, which means the right not to be put on life support, is something we've only had in the United States since 1990. It is a right explicitly granted to us in decisions by the U.S. Supreme Court. Since that time, however, the courts in the different states have made it clear that unless you put your wishes in writing, a doctor does not have to unplug you from life support, no matter how devastated your body is, no matter how much competency you've lost, no matter how much of a vegetable you've become from whatever it is that has befallen you.

The reason this is important to you, not only emotionally but financially, is that most health insurance policies put a cap on the maximum amount they will pay for an illness. This maximum varies from policy to policy, but the average is about $1 million. So, after your insurance company has paid out about $1 million in benefits, it's done. The rest is up to you and your loved ones. With the cost of hospitalization skyrocketing, I am sure you can imagine that it would not take long to reach the maximum if you happened to be on a life-support system in a hospital. And yet the medical bills would keep piling up. Having an advanced health care directive and durable power of attorney for health care is part of being responsible to your family, not only on an emotional level, but on a financial level as well.

An Advanced Directive for Health Care

Also known as a living will, a directive to physicians, a health-care declaration, an advanced health-care directive, or a medical directive, the advanced directive for health care is a written document that dictates what you want to have happen to you if you are incapacitated. You can choose from three basic options:

1. You want to prolong your life for as long as possible, without regard to your con-

dition, your chance of recovery, or the cost of treatment.

2. You want life-sustaining treatment to be provided unless you are in a coma or an ongoing vegetative state.

3. You do not want your life to be prolonged unnaturally, unless there is some hope that both your physical and mental health might be restored.

Durable Power of Attorney for Health Care

A durable power of attorney for health care (which may also be called medical power of attorney, a health care proxy, an appointment of health care agent or surrogate) is a document that designates someone who will have the authority to make health-care decisions if you cannot because of an incapacity. The person appointed may be called a health-care agent, a surrogate, an attorney in-fact, or a proxy. (In Colorado, your agent must be at least 21 years old. In Nebraska, he or she must be at least 19. In all other states, the agent must be 18 or older.)

In the durable power of attorney for heath care, you must decide in whose hands you want to put your life—who, that is, will make the final decision to take you off life support, if the decision ever has to be made. It is best to have an agent and two alternates, in case the person you have chosen is not available. Choose people who love you yet are strong enough to do what you would want them to do. This is not an easy position to be in.

I want you to take a moment to consider who you would want to be the agent and alternates for your durable power of attorney. This is one of the most important decisions you will make, so please do not rush into it. Give it some careful thought, and when you have made up your mind, write the names of your choices in the box on page 90.

> Please locate audio CD "**What You Need to Know Today to Protect Your Tomorrows**," part one. Go to track two, "**Advanced Directive and Durable Power of Attorney for Health Care.**" Follow along on the sample form we have included in your guidebook as Janet and I review these documents. After you have listened to the CD, go to your **Protection Portfolio Forms CD-ROM,** where you will find an advanced directive and power of attorney for health-care document that you can customize to use in any state. You will also find a link to the organization Partnership for Caring, where you can print out copies of your own state's forms. Forms can also be procured at most hospitals or public health services in your area.

ADVANCED DIRECTIVE AND DURABLE POWER OF ATTORNEY

FOR HEALTH CARE

PAGE ONE OF FIVE

Explanation

You have the right to give instructions about your own health care. You also have the right to name someone else to make health-care decisions for you. This form lets you do either or both of these things. It also lets you express your wishes regarding donation of organs. If you use this form, you may complete or modify all or any part of it. You are free to use a different form.

This form is a power of attorney for health care. It lets you name another individual as agent to make health-care decisions for you if you become incapable of making your own decisions or if you want someone else to make those decisions for you now even though you are still capable. You may name an alternate agent to act for you if your first choice is not willing, able, or reasonably available to make decisions for you. (Your agent may not be an operator or employee of a community-care facility or a residential-care facility where you are receiving care or your supervising health-care provider or employee of the health-care institution where you are receiving care, unless your agent is related to you or is a co-worker.)

Unless the form you sign limits the authority of your agent, your agent may make all health-care decisions for you. This form has a place for you to limit the authority of your agent. You need not limit the authority of your agent if you wish to rely on your agent for all health-care decisions that may have to be made. If you choose not to limit the authority of your agent, your agent will have the right to:

(a) Consent or refuse consent to any care, treatment, service, or procedure to maintain, diagnose, or otherwise affect a physical or mental condition;
(b) Select or discharge health-care providers and institutions;
(c) Approve or disapprove diagnostic tests, surgical procedures, and programs of medication;
(d) Direct the provision, withholding, or withdrawal of artificial nutrition and hydration and all other forms of health care, including cardiopulmonary resuscitation; and
(e) Make anatomical gifts, authorize an autopsy, and direct the disposition of your remains.

This form lets you give specific instructions about any aspect of your health care, whether or not you appoint an agent. Choices are provided for you to express your wishes regarding the provision, withholding, or withdrawal of treatment to keep you alive. After completing this form, sign and date the form at the end. The form must be acknowledged before a notary public. Give a copy of the signed and completed form to your physician, to any other health-care providers you may have, to any health-care institution at which you are receiving care, and to any health-care agents you have named. You should talk to the person you have named as agent to make sure that he or she understands your wishes and is willing to take the responsibility.

You have the right to revoke this Advanced Directive Durable Power of Attorney for Health Care or replace this form at any time.

ADVANCED DIRECTIVE AND DURABLE POWER OF ATTORNEY
FOR HEALTH CARE

PAGE TWO OF FIVE

(1) DESIGNATION OF AGENT: I designate the following individual as my agent to make health-care decisions for me:

_____
(Name of individual you choose as agent)

_____   _____   _____ _____
(address)   *(city)*   *(state)* *(zip code)*

_____   _____
(home phone)   *(work phone)*

OPTIONAL: If I revoke my agent's authority or if my agent is not willing, able or reasonably available to make a health-care decision for me, I designate as my first alternate agent:

_____
(Name of individual you choose as first alternative agent)

_____   _____   _____ _____
(address)   *(city)*   *(state)* *(zip code)*

_____   _____
(home phone)   *(work phone)*

OPTIONAL: If I revoke the authority of my agent and first alternate agent or if neither is willing, able or reasonably available to make a health-care decision for me, I designate as my second alternate agent:

_____
(Name of individual you choose as second alternative agent)

_____   _____   _____ _____
(address)   *(city)*   *(state)* *(zip code)*

_____   _____
(home phone)   *(work phone)*

ADVANCED DIRECTIVE AND DURABLE POWER OF ATTORNEY

FOR HEALTH CARE

PAGE THREE OF FIVE

(2) AGENT'S AUTHORITY: My agent is authorized to make all health-care decisions for me, including decisions to provide, withhold, or withdraw artificial nutrition and hydration, and all other forms of health care to keep me alive.

(3) WHEN AGENT'S AUTHORITY BECOMES EFFECTIVE: My agent's authority to make health-care decisions for me takes effect immediately.

(4) AGENT'S OBLIGATION: My agent shall make health-care decisions for me in accordance with this power of attorney for health care, any instructions I give in this form, and my other wishes to the extent known to my agent. To the extent my wishes are unknown, my agent shall make health-care decisions for me in accordance with what my agent determines to be in my best interest. In determining my best interest, my agent shall consider my personal values to the extent known to my agent.

(5) AGENT'S POSTDEATH AUTHORITY: My agent is authorized to make anatomical gifts, authorize an autopsy, and direct disposition of my remains, except as I state here on this form:

_____

_____

_____

(6) NOMINATION OF CONSERVATOR: If a conservator of my person needs to be appointed for me by a court, I nominate the agent designated in this form. If that agent is not willing, able, or reasonably available to act as guardian, I nominate the alternate agents whom I have named, in the order designated.

(7) END-OF-LIFE DECISIONS: I direct that my health-care providers and others involved in my care provide, withhold, or withdraw treatment in accordance with the choice I have marked below: *(Initial only one line)*

_____ **(a)** Choice **NOT** to Prolong Life
    I do not want my life to be prolonged if (1) I have an incurable, and irreversible condition that will result in my death within a relatively short time, (2) I become unconscious and, to a reasonable degree of medical certainty, I will not regain consciousness, or (3) the likely risks and burdens of treatment would outweigh the expected benefits, **OR**

ADVANCED DIRECTIVE AND DURABLE POWER OF ATTORNEY

FOR HEALTH CARE

PAGE FOUR OF FIVE

_____ **(b) Choice to Prolong Life**
I want my life to be prolonged as long as possible within the limits of generally accepted health-care standards.

(8) RELIEF FROM PAIN: I direct that treatment for alleviation of pain or discomfort should be provided at all times even if it hastens my death.

(9) EFFECT OF COPY: A copy of this form has the same effect as the original.

(10) SIGNATURE: Sign and date the form here:

_____   _____
(date)   *(sign your name)*

_____   _____
(address)   *(print your name)*

_____   _____
(city)   *(state)*

State of California
County of _____SS

On this _____ day of _____ in the year _____, before me,
_____ *(insert name of notary public)*
personally appeared _____ *(insert the name of principal)*,
personally known to me (or proved to me on the basis of satisfactory evidence) to be the person whose name is subscribed to this instrument, and acknowledged that he or she executed it. I declare under penalty of perjury that the person whose name is subscribed to this instrument. appears to be of sound mind and under no duress, fraud, or undue influence.

(Notary Seal)

_____
(signature of Notary Public)

ADVANCED DIRECTIVE AND DURABLE POWER OF ATTORNEY

FOR HEALTH CARE

PAGE FIVE OF FIVE

I declare under penalty of perjury that the person who signed this advance health-care directive is personally known to us, or that the signer's identity was proven to us by convincing evidence, (2) that the signer acknowledged this advance directive in my presence, (3) that the individual appears to be of sound mind and under no duress, fraud, or undue influence, (4) that we are not a person appointed as an agent by this advance directive, (5) that we are not the individual's health-care provider, an employee of the individual's health-care provider, the operator or employee of a community-care facility, nor the operator or employee of a residential-care facility for the elderly. We further declare that we are not related to the signer of this advance health care directive by blood, marriage, or adoption, and, to the best of my knowledge, we are not entitled to any part of the estate of the signer when he or she dies.

_____   _____
(date)   (signature of witness)

_____   _____
(address)   (printed name of witness)

_____   _____
(city)   (state)

_____   _____
(date)   (signature of witness)

_____   _____
(address)   (printed name of witness)

_____   _____
(city)   (state)

AGENT AND ALTERNATES FOR DURABLE POWER OF ATTORNEY FOR HEALTH CARE

I will ask _____ to be my agent for my durable power of attorney for health care.

I will ask _____ to be an alternate agent for my durable power of attorney for health care.

I will ask _____ to be an alternate agent for my durable power of attorney for health care.

Once you have decided whom you want to ask, get in touch with your chosen agent and alternates and find a time when you can discuss your decision with them in private. As difficult as this conversation may be, please do not put this step off. The moment you need this document, it's too late to create it.

Financial Power of Attorney

A financial power of attorney is a document that authorizes another person to act for you as if that person were you. This person is called your "agent" or your "attorney-in-fact." You can create a very broad power of attorney, which allows your agent to do things that usually only you can do, such as write checks from your bank accounts, pay your bills, or sign documents on your behalf; alternatively, you can create a very limited power of attorney, which may authorize the agent you name to do just one particular thing for you.

In my opinion, the best power of attorney is one that does the following three things: is authorized by a specific state law (also known as a statutory power of attorney); is a general power of attorney; and survives the incapacity of the maker. These three factors will give you the greatest ease in getting people and

Please go to track three on the audio CD "What You Need to Know Today to Protect your Tomorrows," part one. As you listen to Janet and me discuss "The Financial Power of Attorney," please follow along on the sample form provided below.

After you have listened to the audio CD, follow the directions on the **Protection Portfolio Forms CD-ROM** to customize your own financial power-of-attorney form. You will notice that the form is labeled "California probate code section 4401." Please know that you may use the California form that we are providing in any state; that's because we have included the acknowledgment form and witness forms that are required in states other than California. We have chosen California because it has a specific piece of legislation that makes it possible for you to sue an institution, and have your attorney's fees paid by that institution, if the institution refuses to honor the power of attorney.

Please pay careful attention to the pros and cons of the **"Uniform Statutory Power of Attorney"** form and be especially careful to whom you give this form. I would strongly recommend that you keep it in your Protection Portfolio to be used if and only if you are incapacitated. Otherwise, I would not distribute copies of the power of attorney.

Please note: The agent you appoint must sign the affidavit form provided before using the form if you live in Wisconsin or Pennsylvania.

You must have two witness if you live in Arizona, Arkansas, Connecticut, Washington D.C., Florida, Georgia, Michigan, Ohio, Oklahoma, Pennsylvania, South Carolina, Vermont, or Wisconsin.

If you become incapacitated, the agent must record the original power of attorney at the county recorder's office in North Carolina and South Carolina.

• **How to Sign Documents, Checks, etc.** If your name is John Smith and your agent's name, the person signing for you, is Mary Smith, they sign as follows: *John Smith by his attorney in fact Mary Smith.*

• **Effect of Your Death** After you die, the power of attorney is no longer effective, and the agent should not try to transact any business for you then.

FINANCIAL POWER OF ATTORNEY FORM

California Probate Code Section 4401

NOTICE: THE POWERS GRANTED BY THIS DOCUMENT ARE BROAD AND SWEEPING. THEY ARE EXPLAINED IN THE UNIFORM STATUTORY FROM POWER OF ATTORNEY ACT (CALIFORNIA PROBATE CODE SECTIONS 4400-4465, INCLUSIVE). IF YOU HAVE ANY QUESTIONS ABOUT THESE POWERS, OBTAIN COMPETENT LEGAL ADVICE. THIS DOCUMENT DOES NOT AUTHORIZE ANYONE TO MAKE MEDICAL AND OTHER HEALTH CARE DECISIONS FOR YOU. YOU MAY REVOKE THIS POWER OF ATTORNEY IF YOU LATER WISH TO DO SO.

I, _____

(Your name and address)

appoint _____as my agent (attorney-in-fact) for me in any lawful way with respect to the following initialed subjects

To grant all of the following powers, initial the line in front of (N) and ignore the lines in front of the other powers. To grant one or more, but fewer than all, of the following powers, initial the line in front of each power you are granting. To withhold a power, do not initial the line in front of it. You may, but need not, cross out each power withheld.

Initial

_____ (A) Real Property Transactions
_____ (B) Tangible Personal Property Transactions
_____ (C) Stock and Bond Transactions
_____ (D) Commodity and Option Transactions
_____ (E) Banking and Financial Institution Transactions
_____ (F) Business Operating Transactions
_____ (G) Insurance and Annuity Transactions
_____ (H) Estate, Trust, and Other Beneficiary Transactions
_____ (I) Claims and Litigation
_____ (J) Personal and Family Maintenance.
_____ (K) Benefits from Social Security, Medicare, Medicaid, Governmental Programs
_____ (L) Retirement Plan Transactions
_____ (M) Tax Matters
_____ **(N) ALL OF THE POWERS LISTED ABOVE**

YOU NEED NOT INITIAL ANY OTHER LINES IF YOU INITIAL LINE (N).

FINANCIAL POWER OF ATTORNEY FORM, cont'd

SPECIAL INSTRUCTIONS:
ON THE FOLLOWING LINES, YOU MAY GIVE SPECIAL INSTRUCTIONS LIMITING
OR EXTENDING THE POWERS GRANTED TO YOUR AGENT.

My agent shall have the power to direct distributions of principal from my IRA accounts.

_____

Unless you direct otherwise above, this power of attorney is effective immediately and will continue
until it is revoked. This power of attorney will continue to be effective even though I become
incapacitated. *Strike the preceding sentence if you do not want this power of attorney to continue if you
become incapacitated.*

I agree that any third party who receives a copy of this document may act under it. Revocation of the
power of attorney is not effective as to a third party until the third party has actual knowledge of the
revocation. I agree to indemnify the third party for any claims that arise against the third party because
of reliance on this power of attorney.

Signed this_____day of_____, 20___.

_____   _____
(Your signature)   *(Social Security number)*

BY ACCEPTING OR ACTING UNDER THE APPOINTMENT, THE AGENT ASSUMES
THE FIDUCIARY AND OTHER LEGAL RESPONSIBILITIES OF AN AGENT.

State of   _____
County of   _____ ss.

On _____, 20___ before me, _____, personally appeared _____ proved to
me on the basis of satisfactory evidence to be the person(s) whose name(s) is subscribed to the within
instrument and acknowledged to me that he/she/they executed the same in his/her/their authorized
capacity(ies) and that by his/her/their signature(s) on the instrument the person(s) or the entity upon
behalf of which the person(s) acted, executed the instrument.
WITNESS my hand and official seal.

(Notary Seal)

_____
(Signature of Notary Public)

FINANCIAL POWER OF ATTORNEY FORM, cont'd

I declare under penalty of perjury that the person who signed this power of attorney is personally known to me, or that the Principal's identity was proven to me by convincing evidence, (2) that the Principal acknowledged this power of attorney in my presence, (3) that the individual appears to be of sound mind and under no duress, fraud or undue influence, and (4) that I am not a person appointed as the Attorney in Fact. I further declare that I am not related to the Principal by blood, marriage, or adoption.

_____   _____
(Date)   (Signature of Witness)

_____   _____
(Address)   (Printed name of Witness)

_____   _____
(City)   (State)

_____   _____
(Date)   (Signature of Witness)

_____   _____
(Address)   (Printed name of Witness)

_____   _____
(City)   (State)

FINANCIAL POWER OF ATTORNEY FORM, cont'd

Affidavit power of attorney is in full force

State of _____

County of _____ ss.

_____ being duly sworn, states:
(Print name of Designated Agent)

1. I accept the designation of the Principal appointing me as the Principal's Attorney in Fact under this power of attorney.
2. I have no actual knowledge or notice of a revocation of this power of attorney by death or otherwise.
3. I represent that any third party honoring this power of attorney may rely on this declaration.

_____
(Signature of Attorney in Fact)

Sworn to before me on _____

(Notary Seal)

_____
(Signature of Notary Public)

institutions to cooperate with you when you transact business through a power of attorney. Keep in mind, however, that a general power of attorney has been called a license to steal, since it's like signing a blank check.

Bear in mind that certain institutions may refuse to honor your power of attorney if it is not in the form the institution itself prefers—even if it is a statutory form. The IRS, for example, requires you to use only its form for power of attorney. If you try to limit the scope of your power of attorney or make it too specific, brokerage houses may not want to accept it because they will feel it does not cover all the types of actions they deem necessary. Finally, your power of attorney needs to be "durable"—to remain in effect if you become incapacitated. This is the main reason for any power of attorney.

Your Will

One of the most important steps in being responsible to yourself and others is to make sure that you have a will. Of course, thinking about your death or the death of a family member is no easy assignment, and neither is contemplating a serious illness or incapacity. But planning for the future can, and probably will, give you a sense of control over your life. It's freeing to know that you've protected those you care most about.

I urge you to discuss your estate—the sum total of your property and money—with your spouse or life partner, with your children, and with anyone else who will be financially affected by your death. Also, if you are married or hold joint assets with someone else, please take time now to learn everything you can about your joint finances, so that if you are the one left behind you will not have to cope with financial confusion on top of your grief.

After you've listened to the information on the audio CD, you may have additional questions about wills, so the following section is a resource devoted to what you need to know about wills.

What is a Will?

A will is a legal document that states where you want your assets to go after your death. However, the title to your property will not automatically transfer to your designated beneficiary after your death. Your will must be "probated" in court, which is a lengthy and costly procedure.

What is Probate?

Probate is a court procedure in which the judge first has to authenticate your will and make sure it is valid, then sign a court order to transfer your property over to your beneficiaries. Sounds simple, but in some states it can take six months to two years to complete the process and can be quite expensive. Take California, for example:

Please go to track four on the audio CD **"What You Need to Know Today to Protect Your Tomorrows,"** part one. As you listen to Janet and me discuss a will, please follow along on the sample forms starting on page 103. After you have listened to the CD, then go to the **Protection Portfolio Forms CD-ROM** and customize your will following the directions on the CD-ROM.

Estate Size	Probate Fee, California*
$100,000	$ 8,000
$200,000	$14,000
$300,000	$18,000
$400,000	$22,000
$500,000	$26,000
$600,000	$30,000
$1,000,000	$46,000

* Combined basic fees for executor and attorney.

What is a Probate Affidavit?

If your estate is small, from $5,000 to $100,000 (depending on the state), you might be able to avoid probate with a simple will and a process called probate affidavit. It costs very little, doesn't take much time, and makes it easy for your survivors to receive what you want them to have. Probate affidavit forms are available in most banks at no cost. Be careful, though. Your estate could be worth more than you think.

How Do I Get a Will?

There are a few ways you can do this. You can have a lawyer draw one up. This should cost from a hundred to a few hundred dollars, depending on where you live and how complex your affairs are. You can buy a form will, which should cost about $10, at a stationery store and fill in the blanks, or you can print out the form will from your Protection Portfolio

Forms CD-ROM. If you use any of these methods to draw up your will, you'll also need to sign it and, while you are signing it, have two people witness your signature (unless you live in Vermont, which requires three witnesses) and have them sign the will, too.

Who Can Witness a Will?

A witness must be an adult. A witness must be someone who will not be receiving any gifts in the will. And it is best if a witness is not related to you.

What if I Want to Make Changes to My Will?

Instead of creating a codicil to your will, I recommend that you use the Protection Portfolio to create a new updated will, incorporating the changes you want at this time. This ensures that all of your wishes are contained in a single document.

Terminology of Wills	
TERM	**DEFINITION**
Administrator	When there is no will, this is the person who is appointed by the probate court to collect the assets of the estate, pay its debts, and distribute the rest to beneficiaries.
Beneficiary	A person or organization designated to receive your assets upon your death.
Estate	The sum total of your financial interests, both money and property. Your estate is made up of everything you own at the time of your death, including life insurance, less your outstanding debt.
Executor	The person you appoint in your will to settle your estate. This person will have the administrative responsibility of paying your bills, dealing with the probate court, supervising the process of securing your assets and making sure your wishes are carried out.
Testator	The person who created a will.

Ownership Issues that Affect Property Left by Will

TYPE OF OWNERSHIP	RULES FOR LEAVING PROPERTY
Co-owned property, such as: real estate, cars, securities, small business, copyrights, and other property	If you co-own property, you need to figure out the percentage that you own and if you have the right to gift it to someone else. See rules for leaving co-owned property below.
Property with named beneficiaries such as: life insurance, retirement plans, bank accounts, living trusts	If you named a beneficiary on your account or policy, it will be distributed to that individual, not the beneficiary you named in your will. Please check all of your accounts and policies to make sure you have the correct beneficiary listed.
Property controlled by contract such as: partnership interest, stock in a corporation controlled by share-holder approval	Most contracts dictate how these properties are distributed and in a dispute have preference over your will. See a lawyer if you want to distribute your property differently than as specified in your contract

Rules for Co-Owned Property

HOW PROPERTY IS OWNED	RULES FOR LEAVING PROPERTY
Tenancy in Common	You can give away your share of property unless you are restricted by a contract, a different beneficiary is designated on the account or policy, or marital ownership laws forbid (see rules for married people in community-property and common-law-property states)
Joint Tenancy (also called Joint Tenancy with Right of Survivorship)	You cannot give away your share of joint tenancy property. It automatically goes to any surviving joint tenants.

You may still include joint tenancy property in your will to prepare for the possibility that:
a) the entire property ends up in your estate because the other joint tenants dies before you, or
b) the property is converted to tenancy in common. |
| Tenancy by the Entirety | You cannot give away your share of property held in tenancy by the entirety. It automatically goes to your spouse.

You may include tenancy by the entirety property in your will to prepare for the possibility that:
a) the entire property ends up in your estate because your spouse dies before you, or
b) the property is converted to tenancy in common. |

Rules for Married People in Community Property States
(Community Property states are Arizona, California, Idaho, Nevada, New Mexico, Texas, Washington, Wisconsin)

HOW PROPERTY IS OWNED	RULES FOR LEAVING PROPERTY
Separately	You can give away your separate property, except if: a) the property is held in joint tenancy, or b) the property has a different beneficiary designated on the account or policy, or c) the property is restricted from transfer by a contract
Community Property	You can give away your half of community property, except if: a) the property is held in joint tenancy, or b) the property has a different beneficiary designated on the account or policy, or c) the property is restricted from transfer by a contract

Rules for Married People in Common Law Property States
(Community Property states are ALL states other than Arizona, California, Idaho, Nevada, New Mexico, Texas, Washington, Wisconsin)

HOW PROPERTY IS OWNED	RULES FOR LEAVING PROPERTY
Separate property	You can give away your separate property, except if: a) the property is held in joint tenancy, or b) the property is held in tenancy by the entirety, or c) the property has a different beneficiary designated on the account or policy, or d) the property is restricted from transfer by a contract
Marital Property	You can give away your share of jointly owned property, except if: a) the property is held in joint tenancy, or b) the property is held in tenancy by the entirety, or c) the property has a different beneficiary designated on the account or policy, or d) the property is restricted from transfer by a contract

What is a Holographic Will?

A holographic will is a will you write by hand on a piece of paper; it costs you nothing. Just make sure that the paper you use has no other writing on it or the will won't be considered legal. Make sure, too, that the entire will is in your handwriting and is dated and signed by you. If you make a mistake, don't cross it out. Start over. Anything crossed out makes the will null and void. Do not have anyone witness a holographic will because, again, this will make it null and void. If you want to change a holographic will, you must redo the entire thing. Holographic wills are not legal in every state.

Can Wills Be Contested?

Yes. Anyone who thinks that he or she should have something that the deceased left to someone else in the will has the right to come to court and ask for it. Then the judge has to decide. Also, although people commonly use wills to designate the guardians they want for their children, their recommendation is not binding. It can only express a wish.

How Old Do I Have to Be to Have a Will?

In most states you need to be 18 or older to make a will. In Wyoming you have to be 19 or older. If you are younger than this and think you need a will, see an attorney.

Can I Leave Assets to Beneficiaries Other Than My Spouse and Children?

If you want to leave more than half of your estate to someone other than your spouse, see a lawyer. If you have no spouse and you want to leave more than half of your estate to someone other than your children, see a lawyer.

Can I Leave Assets to Young Beneficiaries?

Most states allow you to leave assets for young people to a custodian to manage until the young person is between 18 and 25, depending on the state. This is called the Uniform Transfers to Minors Act and appears in your will form. Since you can't change the age at which the young person gets the money, as it is set by law, the form uses the maximum age. There are only two states that don't allow this, South Carolina and Vermont. If you are concerned about young beneficiaries in these states, use a trust instead of a will.

What if I Don't Have a Will?

The answer is that you do have a will, whether you know it or not. Even if you haven't personally drawn up a will, the state you live in has something called intestate succession rules. These rules determine exactly who receives any assets held in your name when you die without a written will. Usually, your spouse and children receive your property first; if you aren't survived by a spouse or children, your grandchildren might be next in line, followed by your parents, siblings, nieces, nephews, and cousins. If you die without any relatives whom anyone can find, your assets will pass to the state.

Are There Any Rules about Who Can Be My Executor?

Your executor must be an adult under state law. In the following states, the executor must either be a resident of your state or a relative to be able to waive the bond: Florida, Illinois, Kentucky, Tennessee, Wyoming, Ohio. If you live in Nevada, the executor must be a resident of Nevada. Most wills provide that no bond is required of the executor you name in the will. This saves money.

For additional information about wills, please visit the resource center at *www.suze orman.com.*

Will Beneficiary Statement Examples
Article 2: Gifts of Property – Residue of Estate

In addition to the information supplied on the CD-ROM, I've listed the following will beneficiary statement examples in this guidebook to help make the process of creating your will as easy as possible. With each example, I've highlighted legal terms and listed their definitions. These statements are presented as general guidelines, and when personalizing your will on the CD-ROM, you'll need to modify your statements to fit your circumstances. Please note that the text inside the [BRACKETS] should be changed to reflect the people and/or organizations that you want to name as beneficiaries. The pronouns [he/she] and [his/her] must be changed in all instances to reflect the sex of the designated person.

General instructions and guidelines for creating your will are found on the Protection Portfolio CD-ROM.

TERM	DEFINITION
Right of Representation	This phrase means that if the beneficiary you have named dies before you do, then you want the share that beneficiary would have taken to go to their child or children.
Issue	This phrase means your children, grandchildren, great grandchildren, and/or great great grandchildren. It is also sometimes called your lineal descendants. The definition will include legally adopted issue unless you say that "Issue shall include only natural-born children."

RIGHT of REPRESENTATION and ISSUE EXAMPLE

I leave the residue of my estate to my spouse [SPOUSE'S FULL NAME], if he/she survives me. If my spouse does not survive me by 30 days, then to my children, namely [JANE SMITH], [JOE SMITH], and [ANN SMITH] by right of representation. If my executor determines that a beneficiary's share can be retained for their benefit in a Uniform Transfers to Minor's Act Trust, then the executor shall distribute the beneficiary's share to the executor as custodian under the act to hold said share until the maximum age allowed by law. If I am not survived by issue, then the residue of the Estate shall be distributed, free of trust, to [ORGANIZATION NAME] a tax exempt organization.

TERM	DEFINITION
Equal Shares to Lapse	This phrase means that if one of the beneficiaries dies before you, then their share just goes away, it does not go to their children. So if you give equal shares to seven nieces and nephews and one dies before you, then there will just be six shares even if the deceased nephew had his own children.

Will Beneficiary Statement Examples
Article 2: Gifts of Property – Residue of Estate

EQUAL SHARES to LAPSE EXAMPLE

I leave the residue of my estate to my children, namely [JANE SMITH], [JOE SMITH], and [ANN SMITH] in equal shares. If my executor determines that a beneficiary's share can be retained for their benefit in a Uniform Transfers to Minor's Act Trust, then the executor shall distribute the beneficiary's share to the executor as custodian under the act to hold said share until the maximum age allowed by law.

If any of the children do not survive me for 30 days then their share shall lapse. If I am not survived by any children, then the residue of the Estate shall be distributed, free of trust, in equal shares to my grandchildren, said shares to lapse if any do not survive me.

TERM	DEFINITION
Specific Gifts	Gifts such as this one of your home are usually not the best idea. Since most people don't know when they are going to die, you may have unintended consequences by leaving a specific asset to someone. The asset may have been sold before you die leaving the beneficiary with nothing. You may have spent all your other assets, leaving other beneficiaries with nothing. However, there are cases where it is very clear that specific asset should be given to a specific beneficiary.

SPECIFIC GIFTS EXAMPLE

I distribute the residential real property located at [ADDRESS], [CITY], [STATE] to my [son/daughter] [CHILD'S NAME] who has cared for me for many years. [He/she] shall be responsible for the payment of any mortgage on this property at the time of my death. If my executor determines that a beneficiary's share can be retained for their benefit in a Uniform Transfers to Minor's Act Trust, then the executor shall distribute the beneficiary's share to the executor as custodian under the act to hold said share until the maximum age allowed by law.

If [CHILD'S NAME] does not survive me for 30 days, then this gift shall lapse. The residue of the Estate shall be distributed to my children, namely [CHILD'S NAME], [CHILD'S NAME], and [CHILD'S NAME] by right of representation. If I am not survived by issue, then the residue of the Estate shall be distributed, free of trust, to [ORGANIZATION NAME], a tax exempt organization.

TERM	DEFINITION
Percentages	This phrase means that you can choose to distribute your estate in amounts designated by percentages. This allows you to distribute your estate into equal or unequal shares and between individuals and organizations.

Will Beneficiary Statement Examples
Article 2: Gifts of Property – Residue of Estate

PERCENTAGES EXAMPLE

I leave the residue of my estate to the following beneficiaries in the percentages stated:

Twenty Five Percent (25%) to my [friend/relative] [CAROL FRIEND] by right of representation;

Twenty Five Percent (25%) to my [friend/relative] [JOE FRIEND] and if [he/she] does not survive me for 30 days then [his/her] gift shall lapse and be distributed as part of the balance of the residue;

The balance of the residue of the Estate to [ORGANIZATION NAME] a non-profit organization.

If my executor determines that a beneficiary's share can be retained for their benefit in a Uniform Transfers to Minor's Act Trust, then the executor shall distribute the beneficiary's share to the executor as custodian under the act to hold said share until the maximum age allowed by law.

TERM	DEFINITION
Omit Child	The law presumes that you would never intentionally omit a child from your will or trust. If you have a child whom you do not wish to leave anything to after your death, you must state this fact in your will or trust. "I intentionally leave nothing to my child [CHILD'S NAME]."

OMIT CHILD EXAMPLE

I leave the residue of my estate to my children, namely [JANE SMITH], [JOE SMITH], and [ANN SMITH] in equal shares. I intentionally leave nothing to my child [CHILD'S NAME]. If any of the beneficiaries do not survive me for 30 days then their share shall lapse. If I am not survived by any beneficiaries, then the residue of the Estate shall be distributed, free of trust, in equal shares to [ENTER NAME].

Pour Over Will

Later on, we're going to consider whether you need a revocable living trust and give you directions on how to draw one up. Even if you have a trust, however, you still need a will. In this case, your will takes the form of a "pour over" will. What this means is that any assets that are not owned by you as a trustee of your trust when you die can be added to the trust or "poured" over by your will into your trust. A pour over will covers anything that you might have left out of your trust by mistake.

On pages 105–106, you will find a sample pour over will for a single person and one for a person who is part of a married couple.

SAMPLE OF WILL

WILL OF [YOUR FULL NAME]

I, **[YOUR FULL NAME]**, of [YOUR COUNTY], [YOUR STATE], declare that this is my will. I revoke all prior wills and codicils.

ARTICLE ONE
DECLARATIONS CONCERNING FAMILY AND PROPERTY

1.1 Family. I am married to **[SPOUSE'S FULL NAME]** and I have two children of a prior marriage, namely **[CHILD'S NAME 1]** born July 1, 1992 and **[CHILD'S NAME 2]** born June 5, 1994. I intentionally leave nothing to anyone else claiming to be a child of mine regardless of the validity of their claim.

1.2 Personal Wishes. It is my desire that my executor follow any written directions left with this will regarding memorial services. My remains shall be buried and under no circumstances shall my remains be embalmed.

1.3 Guardian of Person. If it becomes necessary for the court to appoint a guardian of the person for a minor child, I request that the court appoint **[GUARDIAN 1]** or if he/she is unable to act as guardian then **[GUARDIAN 2]** shall be appointed. No bond shall be required of any guardian.

ARTICLE TWO
GIFTS OF PROPERTY

2.1 Tangible Personal Property. I direct my executor to distribute my tangible personal property to my spouse if he/she survives me and if not then to my children in equal shares. I may also leave a non-testamentary letter addressed to the executor requesting that certain of my personal possessions be delivered to named individuals. Although such letter shall not be interpreted as a testamentary writing, I request that my beneficiaries and executor carry out the requests made in the letter. If a minor child is to receive personal property it may be delivered to the child or their guardian or parent as the executor sees fit.

2.2 Residue of Estate. I leave the residue of my estate to my spouse if he/she survives me. If my spouse does not survive me by 30 days, then to my children by right of representation. If my executor determines that a beneficiary's share can be retained for their benefit in a Uniform Transfers to Minor's Act Trust, then the executor shall distribute the beneficiary's share to the executor as custodian under the act to hold said share until the maximum age allowed by law.

If I am not survived by my spouse, my children, or any issue of my children, then the residue of my estate shall be distributed to my siblings who survive me in equal shares, said shares to lapse if any do not survive me.

ARTICLE THREE
APPOINTMENT OF FIDUCIARIES

3.1 Executor. I nominate my spouse to serve as executor of this will. If he/she is unable to serve, then I appoint my sister **[EXECUTOR'S NAME]** to act as executor. If she can not serve and my children are over the age of 25, then they shall act as co-executors. No bond shall be required of any executor under this will.

3.2. Executor's Authority. In addition to any powers and elective rights conferred by statute or federal law or by other provisions of this will, I grant my executor the authority to administer my estate under any procedure for informal or unsupervised administration, or any other available procedure for avoidance of administration or reduction of its burdens.

On _____, 20___ at _____, I hereby sign this document and declare it to be my will.

_____
[YOUR FULL NAME]

This document (consisting of __ pages including this one) was signed and declared to be his/her will by **[YOUR FULL NAME]** in our joint presence. At his/her request, in his/her presence, and in the presence of each other, we hereby sign as witnesses to the execution of this will, believing that he is of sound mind and under no undue influence. Each of us observed the signing of this will by **[YOUR FULL NAME]** and each other subscribing witness and knows that each signature is the true signature of the person whose name was signed. Each of us is now more than eighteen years of age and a competent witness and resides at the address set forth after our name.

We declare under penalty of perjury that the foregoing is true and correct and that this declaration was executed on
_____20___, at _____,
(date)   *(town)*
_____.
(state)

_____, residing at _____
(witness signature)   *(town and state)*

_____, residing at _____
(witness signature)   *(town and state)*

SAMPLE OF SINGLE PERSON POUR OVER WILL

WILL OF [YOUR FULL NAME]

I, [YOUR FULL NAME], of [YOUR COUNTY], [YOUR STATE], declare that this is my will. I revoke all prior wills and codicils.

ARTICLE ONE
DECLARATIONS CONCERNING FAMILY AND PROPERTY

1.1 Family. I am not married. I have one child of a prior marriage, namely [CHILD'S NAME] born March 14, 1988. I intentionally leave nothing to anyone else claiming to be a child of mine regardless of the validity of their claim.

1.2 Personal Wishes. It is my desire that my executor follow any written directions left with this will regarding memorial services. My remains shall be cremated and under no circumstances shall my remains be embalmed.

1.3 Guardian of Person. If it becomes necessary for the court to appoint a guardian of the person for my minor child, I request that the court appoint [GUARDIAN 1] or if he/she is unable to act as guardian then [GUARDIAN 2] shall be appointed. No bond shall be required of any guardian.

ARTICLE TWO
GIFTS OF PROPERTY

2.1 Tangible Personal Property. I direct my executor to distribute my tangible personal property to my daughter if she survives me and if not then as my executor sees fit. I may also leave a non-testamentary letter addressed to the executor requesting that certain of my personal possessions be delivered to named individuals. Although such letter shall not be interpreted as a testamentary writing, I request that my beneficiaries and executor carry out the requests made in the letter. If a minor child is to receive personal property it may be delivered to the child or their guardian or parent as the executor sees fit.

2.2 Residue of Estate. I leave the residue of my estate, to the trustee(s) of the [YOUR FULL NAME] Revocable Trust to be added to that trust and to be held, administered and distributed according to the terms of that trust and any amendments properly made to it.

ARTICLE THREE
APPOINTMENT OF FIDUCIARIES

3.1 Executor. I nominate my daughter [CHILD'S NAME] to serve as executor of this will if she has attained the age of 21. If she does not qualify or ceases to serve, I nominate [EXECUTOR 1] to act as executor and if she can not act, then [EXECUTOR 2] shall act as executor. No bond shall be required of any executor under this will.

3.2. Executor's Authority. In addition to any powers and elective rights conferred by statute or federal law or by other provisions of this will, I grant my executor the authority to administer my estate under any procedure for informal or unsupervised administration, or any other available procedure for avoidance of administration or reduction of its burdens.

On _____ at _____, _____, I hereby sign this document and declare it to be my will.

_____

[YOUR FULL NAME]

This document (consisting of __ pages including this one) was signed and declared to be his/her will by **[YOUR FULL NAME]** in our joint presence. At his request, in his/her presence, and in the presence of each other, we hereby sign as witnesses to the execution of this will, believing that he/she is of sound mind and under no undue influence. Each of us observed the signing of this will by **[YOUR FULL NAME]** and each other subscribing witness and knows that each signature is the true signature of the person whose name was signed.

Each of us is now more than 18 years of age and a competent witness and resides at the address set forth after our name.

We declare under penalty of perjury that the foregoing is true and correct and that this declaration was executed on

_____20___, at _____,
(date)   *(town)*

_____.
(state)

_____, residing at _____
(witness signature)   *(town and state)*

_____, residing at _____

SAMPLE OF A POUR OVER WILL FOR AN INDIVIDUAL WHO IS PART OF A MARRIED COUPLE

WILL OF [YOUR FULL NAME]

I, [YOUR FULL NAME], of [YOUR COUNTY], [YOUR STATE], declare that this is my will. I revoke all prior wills and codicils.

ARTICLE ONE
DECLARATIONS CONCERNING FAMILY AND PROPERTY

1.1 Family. I am married to [SPOUSE'S FULL NAME] and any reference in this will to my spouse is to him/her. We have two children living of our marriage, namely [CHILD'S NAME 1] born March 14, 1992 and [CHILD'S NAME 2] born May 10, 1994. We have one child who died on December 1, 2000, namely [CHILD'S NAME 3] and he/she is survived one child, namely [GRANDCHILD'S NAME] born June 24, 1999. I intentionally leave nothing to anyone else claiming to be a child of mine regardless of the validity of their claim.

1.2 Personal Wishes. It is my desire that my executor follow any written directions left with this will regarding memorial services. My remains shall be cremated and under no circumstances shall my remains be embalmed.

1.3 Guardian of Person. If it becomes necessary for the court to appoint a guardian of the person for my minor child, I request that the court appoint [GUARDIAN 1]. If he/she declines or is unable to act, then [GUARDIAN 2] shall be appointed. No bond shall be required of guardian.

ARTICLE TWO
GIFTS OF PROPERTY

2.1 Tangible Personal Property. I direct my executor to distribute my tangible personal property to my spouse if she survives me and if not then to my children in equal shares. I may also leave a non-testamentary letter addressed to the executor requesting that certain of my personal possessions be delivered to named individuals. Although such letter shall not be interpreted as a testamentary writing, I request that my beneficiaries and executor carry out the requests made in the letter. If a minor child is to receive personal property it may be delivered to the child or their guardian or parent as the executor sees fit.

2.2 Residue of Estate. I leave the residue of my estate, to the trustee(s) of the [YOUR FULL NAME] and [SPOUSE'S FULL NAME] Revocable Trust to be added to that trust and to be held, administered and distributed according to the terms of that trust and any amendments properly made to it.

ARTICLE THREE
APPOINTMENT OF FIDUCIARIES

3.1 Executor. I nominate my spouse [SPOUSE'S FULL NAME] to serve as executor of this will. If he/she does not qualify or ceases to serve, I nominate my children to act as co-executors if they have both attained the age of 18. If they have not attained the age of 18, then my brother [EXECUTOR'S NAME] shall act as executor. No bond shall be required of any executor under this will.

3.2. Executor's Authority. In addition to any powers and elective rights conferred by statute or federal law or by other provisions of this will, I grant my executor the authority to administer my estate under any procedure for informal or unsupervised administration, or any other available procedure for avoidance of administration or reduction of its burdens.

On _____, 20___, at _____, _____, I hereby sign this document and declare it to be my will.

_____
[YOUR FULL NAME]

This document (consisting of __ pages including this one) was signed and declared to be his/her will by **[YOUR FULL NAME]** in our joint presence. At his/her request, in his/her presence, and in the presence of each other, we hereby sign as witnesses to the execution of this will, believing that he/she is of sound mind and under no undue influence. Each of us observed the signing of this will by **[YOUR FULL NAME]** and each other subscribing witness and knows that each signature is the true signature of the person whose name was signed. Each of us is now more than eighteen years of age and a competent witness and resides at the address set forth after our name.

We declare under penalty of perjury that the foregoing is true and correct and that this declaration was executed on

_____20___, at _____,
(date)   *(town)*

_____.
(state)

_____, residing at _____
(witness signature)   *(town and state)*

_____, residing at _____

Will Affidavit

In the past, after you died, in order to prove in probate court that a will was valid, the witnesses who signed the will had to come to court to testify to the fact that they saw you sign the will. Now, in most states, signing such an affidavit can be done ahead of time, at the signing of the will, so witnesses don't have to do anything when you die. In California and Michigan, the form provided here is all that is needed. For other states, please see the forms on the pages that follow.

In the following states, will affidavit form #1 should be added to your will: Alabama, Alaska, Arizona, Arkansas, Colorado, Connecticut, Hawaii, Idaho, Illinois, Indiana, Maine, Minnesota, Mississippi, Montana, Nebraska, Nevada, New Mexico, New York, North Dakota, Oregon, South Carolina, South Dakota, Tennessee, Utah, Washington, and West Virginia.

In the following states, affidavit form #2 should be added to your will: Delaware, Florida, Georgia, Iowa, Kansas, Kentucky, Massachusetts, Missouri, New Jersey, North Carolina, Oklahoma, Pennsylvania, Rhode Island, Virginia, and Wyoming.

In Texas, affidavit form #3 should be added to your will.

In Louisiana, affidavit form #4 should be added to your will.

In New Hampshire, affidavit form #5 should be added to your will.

In Wisconsin, affidavit form #6 should be added to your will.

In Washington D.C., Maryland, Ohio, and Vermont, witnesses can not sign in advance, so you want to make sure that your executor will be able to find your witnesses after you die, in case there is a need to go to court.

Sample Letter to the Executor of Your Will to Add or Change Tangible Personal Property

To avoid having to redo your will every time you change your mind about who you want to receive certain items of personal property, use this informal way of writing a letter to your will's executor. If you write directions in your own handwriting, it makes your letter a stronger statement. Typically, you will direct some of your possessions to specific people; almost never will you direct the disposition of each and every thing.

Tangible personal property includes your furniture, jewelry, artwork, personal papers, cars, tools, clothes, computers, appliances, cameras, electronic equipment, pets, etc.

State Guidelines for Probate

Whether you need only a will or a revocable living trust, to avoid probate depends on the state in which you live, the size of your probate estate, and which assets you are leaving to your beneficiaries. If the assets you want to leave are larger than allowed for below, you should seriously consider a revocable living trust.

The following guidelines are based on state laws for informal probate. Informal probate is cheaper and faster than full probate but can usually only be used when there are no disagreements among the inheritors. Sometimes this procedure is limited to spouses and children. If your state allows informal probate, then you may not need a trust, so the dollar amounts below are based on limits for informal probate. That said, however, there are some additional considerations that may indicate the use of trust.

Consider a trust if:
- there is a possibility that there will be beneficiaries under the age of 25; if so, use a trust.
- you have children with special needs, meaning that they will never be able to support themselves financially due to a physical or mental disability.
- you own real estate of any value in more than one state.
- your estate is worth close to $1,000,000; if this is true of you, have a trust prepared by an experienced trust lawyer.

WILL AFFIDAVIT

Affidavit Will Form #1

For the following states: Alabama, Alaska, Arizona, Arkansas, Colorado, Connecticut, Hawaii, Idaho, Illinois, Indiana, Maine, Minnesota, Mississippi, Montana, Nebraska, Nevada, New Mexico, New York, North Dakota, Oregon, South Carolina, South Dakota, Tennessee, Utah, Washington, and West Virginia.

We, _____,

(Print name of Testator)

_____, and _____,

(Print name of Witness)   *(Print name of Witness)*

the testator and the witnesses, whose names are signed to the attached instrument in those capacities, personally appearing before the undersigned authority and being first duly sworn, declare to the undersigned authority under penalty of perjury that:

1) the testator declared, signed and executed the instrument as his or her last will;
2) he or she signed it willingly or directed another to sign for him or her;
3) he or she executed it as his or her free and voluntary act for the purposes therein expressed; and
4) each of the witnesses, at the request of the testator, in his or her hearing and presence, and in the presence of each other, signed the will as witness and that to the best of his or her knowledge the testator was at that time of full legal age, of sound mind and under no constraint or undue influence.

Testator: _____

(Signature of Testator)

Witness: _____

(Signature of Witness)

Address: _____

Witness: _____

(Signature of Witness)

Address: _____

Subscribed, sworn and acknowledged before me, _____, a Notary Public, by _____, the testator, and by _____, and _____, the witnesses, this _____ day of _____, 20___.

(Notary Seal)

Signature of Notary Public _____

My commission expires:_____

WILL AFFIDAVIT

Affidavit Will Form #2

For use in the following states: Delaware, Florida, Georgia, Iowa, Kansas, Kentucky, Massachusetts, Missouri, New Jersey, North Carolina, Oklahoma, Pennsylvania, Rhode Island, Virginia, and Wyoming.

State of _____

County of _____

I, the undersigned, an officer authorized to administer oaths, certify that We,

_____ ,the testator, and

(Print name of Testator)

_____ , and _____ ,

(Print name of Witness)   *(Print name of Witness)*

the witnesses, whose names are signed to the attached or foregoing instrument and whose signatures appear below, having appeared together before me and having been first duly sworn, each then declared to me that:

1) the attached or foregoing instrument is the last will of the testator;
2) the testator willingly and voluntarily declared, signed and executed the will in the presence of the witnesses;
3) the witnesses signed the will upon request by the testator, in the presence and hearing of the testator, and in the presence of each other;
4) to the best knowledge of each witness the testator was, at that time of the signing, of the age of majority (or otherwise legally competent to make a will), of sound mind, and under no constraint or undue influence; and
5) each witness was and is competent, and of the proper age to witness a will.

Testator: _____

      (Signature of Testator)

Witness: _____

      (Signature of Witness)

Address: _____

Witness: _____

      (Signature of Witness)

Address: _____

Subscribed, sworn and acknowledged before me, _____ , a Notary Public, by _____ , the testator, and by _____ , and _____ , the witnesses, this _____ day of _____ , 20 ____ .

Signed: _____

_____
(Official Capacity of Officer)

WILL AFFIDAVIT

Affidavit Will Form #3
For Texas Only

The State of Texas
County of _____

Before me, the undersigned authority, on this day personally appeared

_____,the testator, and
(Print name of Testator)

_____, and _____,
(Print name of Witness)   *(Print name of Witness)*

known to me to be the testator and the witnesses, respectively, whose names are subscribed to the annexed or foregoing instrument in their respective capacities, and, all of said persons being by me duly sworn, the said _____, testator, declared to me and to the said witnesses in my presence that said instrument is his or her last will and testament, and that he or she had willingly made and executed it as his or her free act and deed; and the said witnesses, each on his or her oath stated to me, in the presence and hearing of the said testator, that the said testator had declared to them that said instrument is his or her last will and testament, and that he or she executed same as such and wanted each of them to sign it as a witness; and upon their oaths each witness stated further that they did sign the same as witnesses in the presence of the said testator and at his or her request; that he or she was at the time eighteen years of age or over (or being under such age, was or had been lawfully married, or was then a member of the armed forces of the United States or an auxiliary thereof or of the Maritime Service) and was of sound mind; and that each of said witnesses was then at least 14 years of age.

Testator: _____
                (Signature of Testator)

Witness: _____
                (Signature of Witness)

Witness: _____
                (Signature of Witness)

Subscribed and sworn to before me by the said

_____, testator, and by the said
_____, and
_____ witnesses,
this _____ day of _____, 20___.

(Notary Seal)

Signed: _____

_____
(Official Capacity of Officer)

WILL AFFIDAVIT

Affidavit Will Form #4
For Louisiana Only

State of _____
County of _____

In our presence, the testator has declared or signified that this instrument is his testament and has signed it at the end and on each other separate page, and in the presence of the testator and each other, we have hereunto subscribed our names this _____ day of _____, 20____.

Witness: _____
         (Witness signature)

Witness: _____
         (Witness signature)

Subscribed and sworn to before me by _____, the testator, and by, _____, and _____, witnesses,

this day of _____, 20____.

(Notary Seal)

Signed: _____
_____
(Official Capacity of Officer)

WILL AFFIDAVIT

Affidavit Will Form #5
For New Hampshire Only

The foregoing instrument was acknowledged before me this _____ (day) by
_____, the testator; _____ and
(Testator signature)   *(Witness signature)*

_____, the witnesses, who under oath do swear as follows:
(Witness signature)

1. The testator signed the instrument as the testator's will or expressly directed another to sign for the testator.
2. This was the testator's free and voluntary act for the purposes expressed in the will.
3. Each witness signed at the request of the testator, in the testator's presence, and in the presence of the other witness.
4. To the best of my knowledge, at the time of the signing the testator was at least 18 years of age, or if under 18 years was a married person, and was of sane mind and under no constraint or undue influence.

(Notary Seal)

Signed: _____

_____
(Official Capacity of Officer)

WILL AFFIDAVIT

Affidavit Will Form #6
For Wisconsin Only

State of _____

County of _____

I, _____, the testator, sign my name to this instrument this day of

(Print name of Testator)

_____ _____, and being first duly sworn, declare to the undersigned authority all of the

following:

1. I execute this instrument as my will.
2. I sign this will willingly, or willingly direct another to sign for me.
3. I execute this will as my free and voluntary act for the purposes expressed therein.
4. I am 18 years of age or older, of sound mind, and under no constraint or undue influence.

Testator: _____

(Testator signature)

We, _____, _____, the witnesses, being first duly sworn,

(Print name of Witness)   *(Print name of Witness)*

sign our names to this instrument and declare to the undersigned authority all of the following:

1. The testator executes this instrument as his or her will.
2. The testator signs it willingly, or willingly directs another to sign for him or her.
3. Each of us, in the conscious presence of the testator, signs this will as a witness.
4. To the best of our knowledge, the testator is 18 years of age or older, of sound mind, and under no
constraint or undue influence.

Witness: _____

(Witness signature)

Witness: _____

(Witness signature)

Subscribed and sworn to before me by _____, the testator, and by

_____, and _____, witnesses, this day of

_____, 20___.

(Notary Seal)

Signed: _____

_____

(Official Capacity of Officer)

SAMPLE LETTER TO EXECUTOR TO ADD OR CHANGE PERSONAL PROPERTY

February 15, 2002

Dear Mr. Smith, executor of my will dated_____:

Please give my 1956 Chevrolet car to my grandson John Smith.

Please give my wedding ring, gold jewelry, and watch to my daughter Mary.

Please give my tools and computers to my son John.

Please give my collection of china and crystal to my friend Linda Smith.

Yours,

_____ Name

_____ Signature

There are many special rules for simplified court procedures between spouses. However, if your spouse's and your assets exceed the guidelines set forth below, I recommend that you do a joint trust, so you are protected if you die together or die within a year or so of each other.

ALABAMA Use a trust if the net estate is worth more than $3,000.

ALASKA Use a trust if the net estate is worth more than $250,000.

ARIZONA Use a trust if the net estate is worth more than $100,000 or real estate is worth more than $50,000.

ARKANSAS Use a trust if you have more than a principal residence and $50,000.

CALIFORNIA Use a trust if you have real estate worth more than $20,000 or assets other than real estate worth more than $100,000.

COLORADO Use a trust if the net estate is worth more than $27,000.

CONNETICUT Use a trust if you own real estate. If you don't own real estate, use a trust if the value of the net estate exceeds $20,000.

DELAWARE Use a trust if you own real estate. If you don't own real estate, use a trust if the total value of the net estate exceeds $20,000.

DISTRICT OF COLUMBIA Use a trust if your assets are worth more than $40,000.

FLORIDA Use a trust if you own real estate or the value of the net estate exceeds $60,000.

GEORGIA Use a trust unless you do not wish to make distributions to anyone but your heirs at law, you know that there will be no arguments, and you know you will have no debts when you die.

HAWAII Use a trust if you own real estate or if the value of all assets other than real estate is more than $100,000. Court will take 3% of assets transferred under $100,000 as a fee.

IDAHO Use a trust if the value of the net estate exceeds $50,000 and there is no real estate.

ILLINOIS Use a trust if the value of the net estate exceeds $50,000.

INDIANA Use a trust if the value of the net estate exceeds $25,000.

IOWA Use a trust if the value of the net estate exceeds $50,000 or if you are leaving assets of more than $15,000 to someone other than a spouse or child.

KANSAS Use a trust if value of the net estate exceeds $20,000 and includes real estate.

(The simplified probate procedures are generous in Kansas, but they depend on approval of a judge, so there are no consistent guidelines.)

KENTUCKY Use a trust if value of net estate exceeds $7,500.

LOUISIANA Use a trust if you own real estate or other assets worth more than $50,000, or if you want to leave assets to someone other than a family member. (Executor gets a minimum of 2.5% of estate value.)

MAINE Use a trust if value of net estate exceeds $60,000.

MARYLAND Use a trust if value of net estate exceeds $30,000.

MASSACHUSETTS Use a trust if value of net estate exceeds $15,000.

MICHIGAN Use a trust if value of net estate exceeds $15,000

MINNESOTA Use a trust if value of net estate is over $20,000 or you own real estate.

MISSISSIPPI	Use a trust if value of net estate is over $500.
MISSOURI	Use a trust if value of net estate is over $40,000.
MONTANA	Use a trust if value of net estate is over $60,000.
NEBRASKA	Use a trust if value of net estate is over $12,500.
NEVADA	Use a trust if value of net estate is over $50,000.
NEW HAMPSHIRE	Use a trust if value of net estate is over $10,000 or if you own real estate.
NEW JERSEY	Use a trust if value of net estate is over $5,000.
NEW MEXICO	Use a trust if the net estate is worth more than $30,000 or if there is any real estate.
NEW YORK	Use a trust if value of net estate exceeds $20,000 or includes real estate.
NORTH CAROLINA	Use a trust if value of net estate exceeds $10,000 or includes real estate.
NORTH DAKOTA	Use a trust if value of net estate exceeds $80,000.
OHIO	Use a trust if value of net estate exceeds $35,000.
OKLAHOMA	Use a trust if value of net estate exceeds $60,000.
OREGON	Use a trust if value of net estate exceeds $140,000 or you own real estate worth more than $90,000.
PENNSYLVANIA	Use a trust if value of net estate exceeds $25,000 or you own real estate.
RHODE ISLAND	Use a trust if value of net estate exceeds $15,000 or you own real estate.
SOUTH CAROLINA	Use a trust if value of net estate exceeds $10,000.
SOUTH DAKOTA	Informal probate is available regardless of value of net estate, so use a trust if there is a possibility that your beneficiaries will not all agree on how to distribute your assets.
TENNESSEE	Use a trust if value of net estate exceeds $25,000 or includes real estate.
TEXAS	Informal probate available regardless of value of net estate, but inheritors must all agree so use a trust if there is a possibility that your beneficiaries will not all agree on how to distribute your assets. Must authorize independent administrator in the will. Still have to do several filings with the court for informal probate.
UTAH	Use a trust if value of net estate exceeds $20,000.
VERMONT	Use a trust if value of net estate exceeds $10,000 or includes real estate.
VIRGINIA	Use a trust. There is no provision for informal probate.
WASHINGTON	Informal probate available regardless of value of net estate so use a trust if there is a possibility that your beneficiaries will not all agree on how to distribute your assets. Still have to do several filings with the court for informal probate.
WEST VIRGINIA	Use a trust if value of net estate it more than $100,000 or you own real estate.
WISCONSIN	Use a trust if value of net estate is more than $50,000 or if you are leaving assets to someone other than a spouse and children.
WYOMING	Use a trust if value of net estate exceeds $70,000.

Revocable Living Trusts

Please go to track two on the audio CD **"What You Need to Know Today to Protect your Tomorrows,"** part two. As you listen to Janet and I discuss a trust, please follow along on the sample forms provided on pages 128–133.

Of all the documents I have ever talked to you about, of all the things you have ever heard me mention on television or in any book, a revocable living trust is the document I have probably most often said is indispensable. It is certainly one of the most important documents you can have to protect yourself.

Before I describe in detail what a revocable living trust is and what it can do for you, please take the following quiz:

TEST YOURSELF
Do I Need a Trust to Avoid Probate?

To determine if you need a trust, add up your estate's assets below:

Estate Assets	Value of Estate Assets
Residence	_____
Life insurance death benefit	_____
Real estate other than home	_____
Cars	_____
Business interests	_____
(limited partnership, LLC, S Corp.)	
Investments	_____
(stocks, bonds, mutual funds)	
Retirement plans	_____
with death benefits	
(IRA, Keogh, 401(k), 403(b), 457)	
Bank accounts	_____

Total Estimated Value of Estate

Please answer yes or no.

	YES	NO
Is the estimated value of your estate less than your state maximum amount to avoid probate?	❏	❏

If you answered yes in the box above, then you do not need a revocable living trust to avoid probate. But there may still be other reasons for you to have a trust.

Who Should Have a Trust?

Please answer yes or no to the following questions.

	YES	NO
Do you have a financial interest in a business?	❏	❏
Do you have children?	❏	❏
Are you in a second or third marriage?	❏	❏
Are you on bad terms with one or more of your heirs?	❏	❏
Are any family members physically ill?	❏	❏
Is any family member mentally ill?	❏	❏
Is any family member developmentally disabled?	❏	❏
Is any family member in need of creditor protection?	❏	❏
Is any family member bad at managing money?	❏	❏

If you answered yes to any of the above questions, then you should seriously consider establishing a trust.

After you listen to the information about trusts on the audio CD, you may have additional questions. The following section is an added resource devoted to what you need to know about trusts.

What is a Revocable Living Trust?

A revocable living trust is a written document stating who controls your assets while you are alive (typically, you) and what will happen to those assets once you are gone. It is called "revocable" because you can change

Terminology of Trusts	
Term	**Definition**
Beneficiary	A person or organization designated to receive your assets upon your death.
Current Beneficiary	The person or persons for whom all assets are being held in trust.
Estate	The sum total of your financial interests, both money and property. Your estate is made up of everything you own at the time of your death, including life insurance, less your outstanding debt.
Remainder Beneficiaries	The person or persons who will inherit everything in the trust after the current beneficiary (who is usually the trustor as well) dies.
Successor Trustee	The person who steps in to make decisions about the assets in the trust if and only if the trustee or co-trustees cannot or do not want to act in the decision-making process.
Settlor, Trustor, or Grantor	The person who creates a trust and owns the property that will be put into the trust.
Trustee	The person or group of persons who control the assets in the trust. Most often the trustor is also the trustee. When you set up a trust, you do not have to give away your power over your assets. Most people continue taking care of everything just as they did before the trust existed.

it at any time; "living" because you create and fund it while you are alive; and a "trust" because you entrust it with the title to your property. Its purpose is to hold your assets while you live and carry out your wishes when you can no longer do so for yourself.

How is a Revocable Living Trust Different from a Will?

Revocable trusts are an increasingly popular alternative to wills. Although a will states to whom you want your assets to go after your death, it takes effect only with a court order. With a revocable living trust, the court is removed from the equation. You take the necessary actions while you are alive to pass assets directly to your beneficiaries once you die. You do this by signing the title of your

assets over to the trust. The property is held in your name—as trustee for your trust—and for your benefit while you live. You can always add things to the trust, take things out of it, and amend it if you change your mind about who you wish to get what. When you die the trust passes your property directly to the people you want to have it. And it does so without probate.

What is the Cost of a Revocable Living Trust?

Depending on the size of your estate, you should be able to get a simple revocable living trust drawn up by an attorney for between $500 and $3,000. If you decide you want the attorney to fund the trust—that is, to transfer your assets into it—it might cost you more. Once the trust is set up, making simple changes to it should cost about $100. Obviously, fees will vary depending on the state where you live and how complex your requirements are.

What Is "Funding" a Trust?

Funding the trust means transferring the title to assets into the trust. By itself, the trust document means nothing; it's only when the trust assumes ownership of the things you intend to put into it that it becomes a useful financial tool.

Here's an example of funding a trust. Let's say that John and Jane Doe own a house together in their own names. They decide to create and fund a trust to hold the title to their house and other assets. After they have established the trust, they would record a new deed that would list the owner of the house as John and Jane Doe, trustees for the John and Jane Doe Revocable Trust. The house would then be "in" the trust. The Does could also change the titles on their bank accounts, stock brokerage account, and so on, so that these were also held by the trust. Doing all this is simply a matter of paperwork.

That said, different institutions have different requirements for making the change of title, so it could be advantageous to have your lawyer handle funding the trust for you. A thorough attorney will update the beneficiary designations on your life insurance policies and your IRAs and other retirement accounts at the same time.

On pages 143–152 there are sample forms used to fund a trust.

How Do You Provide for Children with a Trust?

If you have children, the earlier you create your revocable living trust the better. That's true even if you don't have a lot of money. If your children are very young and if anything were to happen to you, they might be at greater risk than you imagine. A court always has the last word when it comes to who is appointed legal guardian of your children; a will can only express your wishes. So, for example, if your children are under 18 and all you leave them is a life insurance policy, a guardianship for those assets will be created upon your death. Each year the guardian will have to go back to court to account for the money spent on behalf of the children. When each child reaches 18, that child's share will be legally signed over to him or her, lock, stock, and barrel, regardless of his or her ability to handle the money. But by the time the children get the money, there will not be as much of it as there could have been, since every year there will have been guardian fees and fees to a lawyer to do the guardianship reporting. These fees are usually in the thousands of dollars.

Trusts don't address the issue of guardianship (you need a will for that). But if you die with a trust, you do get to make the important decision of how, when, and for what purposes your children will receive the money you are leaving them. You can assign one or more successor trustees (your chosen guardian, for example) and instruct him or them to carry out your wishes as to when your children should receive their money and how that money should be used until that time—and poof, it's done. The successor trustee(s) can take care of your children's financial lives on your behalf. No yearly court reporting, no fees.

Will a Revocable Living Trust Help Me with Estate Taxes?

No. A revocable living trust will not help with the estate taxes on estates whose value rises above the unified credit exemption. A revocable living trust is primarily helpful in transferring legal title to your assets as quickly as possible to beneficiaries, eliminating probate fees, and protecting you when you become incapacitated by providing for a smooth transition of management to your successor trustee without the need for court involvement.

What is the Unified Credit Exemption?

It is the amount that your beneficiaries can inherit from you without having to pay federal estate taxes, as follows:

Due to the Economic Growth and Tax Relief Reconciliation Act of 2001, beginning in 2002 estate taxes are being phased out over nine years. According to the law as it now stands, if you die in the year 2010 there will be no estate tax due on your estate, no matter what its size; and the top gift-tax rate will be equal to the highest individual income-tax rate (scheduled to be 35 percent), with a $1,000,000 unified credit exemption. But please keep in mind that in 2011, unless new legislation is passed, the act will expire and estate taxes, along with the highest unified credit exemption, will be reinstated at the 2001 rate.

Unified Credit Exemption

For Deaths Occurring In	Highest Estate Exemption	Highest Estate & Gift Tax Rate
2002	$1,000,000	50%
2003	$1,000,000	49%
2004	$1,500,000	48%
2005	$1,500,000	47%
2006	$2,000,000	46%
2007	$2,000,000	45%
2008	$2,000,000	45%
2009	$3,500,000	45%

Is There Any Trust that Reduces Estate Taxes?

Yes. An A-B trust (also known as a tax-planning trust, a credit-shelter trust, a marital trust, or a bypass trust) reduces estate taxes. If you have close to $1 million in assets, I urge you to see a trust attorney about an A-B trust.

NEED TO KNOW

Explanation of the Use of a California Trust

You may have noticed that the trust provides that it's governed by the laws of the state of California. This means that no matter which state you live in, California law will be applied to the interpretation of your trust. California trust law is very modern and user friendly, and the laws of California are more favorable to the consumer than those of any other state, in my opinion.

The reason that your trust is valid in your home state, even though it's governed by California law, is based on the same laws that allow a person to incorporate in Delaware even if they've never set foot in that state. The specifics of this principle are found in section 268(1) of the *Restatement of the Law Second, Conflict Laws,* (St. Paul, Minn.: American Law Institute Publishers, 1969) which states:

"As with testamentary trusts, a settlor may designate which state's local law will govern construction of the terms of the trust regardless of whether or not the designated state has any connection with the trust."

How Do I Find a Good Will and Trust Attorney?

This is the hardest part of creating a will and a trust: finding a good will and trust attorney. Word of mouth is the age-old method of choice; so ask your friends, but please be certain that the attorney you choose is well versed in estate planning. If friends can't recommend a qualified attorney, you might want to contact your local university, especially if it has a law school. Call and ask a professor who specializes in estate planning whom he or she would recommend.

Alternatively, you can consult this professional organization:

The American College of
   Trust and Estate Counsel
3415 South Sepulveda Boulevard, Suite 460
Los Angeles, CA 90034
(310) 398-1888
(310) 572-7280 (fax)
www.actec.org

After you've collected some names, please make sure you interview at least three attorneys. Good attorneys are usually too busy for full interviews but most will give you an interview by phone. An attorney will play a major role in making sure your estate is set up correctly, and your survivor will need his or her assistance after your death. You want to be sure that not only you but also those around you like this lawyer and feel comfortable in his or her presence.

How to Interview a Will and Trust Attorney

Ask a prospective attorney the following questions, and be sure you get the following answers before going further. If you get another answer, you haven't found the right attorney:

- **How long have you been specializing in estate planning?** The only acceptable answer is at least ten years.

- **What other areas of law do you practice?** The answer should be no other areas.

- **How many people have you drafted wills and trusts for in the past five years?** The only acceptable answer is at least 200 people.

- **Will you be drafting the documents yourself, or will someone else be doing the paperwork?** It is okay if someone else draws up the documents, as long as that person is supervised correctly. In fact, this arrangement may cost you less. You just need to know one way or the other.

- **How much do you charge?** You want the attorney to charge a flat fee to draw up a will and/or a trust. The fee should include drafting and explaining the document (which could take a few hours if it is a trust), as well as funding the trust (doing the paperwork to transfer the titles on all your property and assets into the name of the trust).

- **If I have other questions, will you charge me if I call and ask?** There should be no charge for simple questions over the phone.

On the next page, you will find a worksheet to use when you are interviewing prospective attorneys. Remember, you need to interview at least three attorneys before you decide.

Find an Attorney Worksheet

Company name:

Company phone number:

Company address:

Contact:

How long have you been specializing in estate planning?

Do you practice in other areas of the law?

How many people have you drafted wills and trusts for in the past five years?

Will you be drafting the documents yourself, or will someone else be doing the paperwork?

How much do you charge?

If I have other questions, will you charge me if I call and ask?

Company name:

Company phone number:

Company address:

Contact:

How long have you been specializing in estate planning?

Do you practice in other areas of the law?

How many people have you drafted wills and trusts for in the past five years?

Will you be drafting the documents yourself, or will someone else be doing the paperwork?

How much do you charge?

If I have other questions, will you charge me if I call and ask?

Trust Beneficiary Statement Examples
Article 6: Distribution of the Trust – Residue of Estate

In addition to the information supplied on the CD-ROM, I've listed the following trust beneficiary statement examples in this guidebook to help make the process of creating your will as easy as possible. With each example, I've highlighted legal terms and listed their definitions. These statements are presented as general guidelines, and when personalizing your trust on the CD-ROM, you'll need to modify your statements to fit your circumstances. Please note that the text inside the [BRACKETS] should be changed to reflect the people and/or organizations that you want to name as beneficiaries. The pronouns [he/she] and [his/her] must be changed in all instances to reflect the sex of the designated person.

General instructions and guidelines for creating your trust are found on the Protection Portfolio CD-ROM.

TERM	DEFINITION
Parent Support	If you use this choice, the parent beneficiary may not serve as your Trustee or Sucessor Trustee. Please refer to the audio CD for more information regarding Parent Support provisions.

PARENT SUPPORT EXAMPLE

The Trustee shall retain twenty five percent (25%) of the Trust Estate in trust for the benefit of [FATHER'S/MOTHER'S NAME], [father/mother] of the Settlor. The Trustee shall pay such sums from the income and principal of this trust share for the benefit of the Settlor's [father/mother] as the Trustee deems appropriate. The beneficiary shall have no right to demand any distribution from this trust share and the existence of this trust share shall not be included as a resource of the beneficiary for the purposes of determining [his/her] eligibility based on financial need for any program or benefit. Upon the death of [FATHER'S/MOTHER'S NAME] the balance then remaining of this share shall be distributed as part of the residue of the Trust Estate. Under no circumstances may the parent, [FATHER'S/MOTHER'S NAME], serve as the Trustee for this trust share.
The residue of the Trust Estate shall be distributed, free of trust, to [CHILD'S NAME], [son/daughter] of the Settlors, by right of representation, subject to the provisions set forth in paragraph B herein below. If [CHILD'S NAME] does not survive the Settlors and leaves no issue, then the residue of the Trust Estate shall be distributed to [BENEFICIARY 1] and [BENEFICIARY 2] by right of representation.

TERM	DEFINITION
Right of Representation	This phrase means that if the beneficiary you have named dies before you do, then you want the share that beneficiary would have taken to go to their child or children.
Issue	This phrase means your children, grandchildren, great grandchildren, and/or great great grandchildren. It is also sometimes called your lineal descendants. The definition will include legally adopted issue unless you say that, "Issue shall include only natural-born children."

Trust Beneficiary Statement Examples
Article 6: Distribution of the Trust – Residue of Estate

RIGHT of REPRESENTATION and ISSUE EXAMPLE

The Trustee shall distribute the residue of the Trust Estate to the Settlors' children, namely [JANE SMITH], [JOE SMITH], AND [ANN SMITH] by right of representation. If the Settlors are not survived by issue, then the residue of the Trust Estate shall be distributed, free of trust, to [ORGANIZATION NAME] a tax exempt organization.

TERM	DEFINITION
Equal Shares to Lapse	This phrase means if one of the beneficiaries dies before you, then their share just goes away, it does not go to their children. So if you give equal shares to seven nieces and nephews and one dies before you, then there will just be six shares even if the deceased nephew had his own children.

EQUAL SHARES to LAPSE EXAMPLE

The Trustee shall distribute the residue of the Trust Estate to the Settlor's children, namely [JANE SMITH], [JOE SMITH], and [ANN SMITH] in equal shares. If any of the children do not survive the Settlor for 30 days then their share shall lapse. If the Settlor is not survived by any children, then the residue of the Trust Estate shall be distributed, free of trust, in equal shares to the Settlor's grandchildren, said shares to lapse if any do not survive the settlor.

TERM	DEFINITION
Specific Gifts	Gifts (such as this one of your home) are usually not the best idea. Since most people don't know when they are going to die, leaving a specific asset to someone may have unintended consequences. The asset may have been sold before you die, leaving the beneficiary with nothing. You may have spent all your other assets, leaving other beneficiaries with nothing. However, there are cases where it is very clear that a specific asset should be given to a specific beneficiary.

Trust Beneficiary Statement Examples
Article 6: Distribution of the Trust – Residue of Estate

SPECIFIC GIFTS EXAMPLE

The Trustee shall distribute the residential real property located at [ADDRESS], [CITY], [STATE] to our [son/daughter] [CHILD'S NAME] who has cared for us for many years. [He/she] shall be responsible for the payment of any mortgage on this property at the time of my death. If [CHILD'S NAME] does not survive the Settlors for 30 days then this gift shall lapse. The residue of the Trust Estate shall be distributed to our children, namely [CHILD'S NAME], [CHILD'S NAME], and [CHILD'S NAME] by right of representation. If the Settlors are not survived by issue, then the residue of the Trust Estate shall be distributed, free of trust, to [ORGANIZATION NAME], a tax exempt organization.

TERM	DEFINITION
Percentages	This phrase means that you can choose to distribute your estate in amounts designated by percentages. This allows you to distribute the residue of the Trust into equal or unequal shares and between individuals and organizations.

EQUAL SHARES to LAPSE EXAMPLE

The Trustee shall distribute the residue of the Trust Estate as follows:
Twenty Five Percent (25%) to my [friend/relative] [CAROL FRIEND] by right of representation;
Twenty Five Percent (25%) to my [friend/relative] [JOE FRIEND] and if [he/she] does not survive me for 30 days then [his/her] gift shall lapse and be distributed as part of the balance of the residue;
The balance of the residue of the Trust Estate to [ORGANIZATION NAME] a non-profit organization.

TERM	DEFINITION
Omit Child	The law presumes that you would never intentionally omit a child from your will or trust. If you have a child whom you do not wish to leave anything to after your death, you must state this fact in your will or trust." intentionally leave nothing to my child [CHILD'S NAME]."

OMIT CHILD EXAMPLE

The Trustee shall distribute the residue of the trust Estate to the Settlor's children, namely [JANE SMITH], [JOE SMITH], and [ANN SMITH] in equal shares. We intentionally leave nothing to our child [CHILD'S NAME]. If any of the beneficiaries do not survive the Settlor for 30 days then their share shall lapse. If the Settlor is not survived by beneficiaries then the residue of the Trust Estate shall be distributed, free of trust, in equal shares to [ENTER NAME].

SAMPLE SINGLE PERSON REVOCABLE TRUST

[YOUR FULL NAME] REVOCABLE TRUST

ARTICLE ONE

This trust agreement, executed _____, 20___ is between **[YOUR FULL NAME]**, as Settlor and **[YOUR FULL NAME]** as Trustee. The Settlor has transferred or will transfer property to the Trustee, which shall be held, in trust, on the terms set forth in this agreement.

ARTICLE TWO

A. Property subject to this instrument is referred to as the Trust Estate and shall be held, administered, and distributed in accordance with this instrument.

B. Other property acceptable to the Trustee may be added to the Trust Estate by any person, by the Will or Codicil of the Settlor, by the proceeds of any life insurance or otherwise.

C. All the property in this trust is the separate property of the Settlor and there is no community or marital property interest in the Trust Estate.

ARTICLE THREE

A. While living and competent, the Settlor reserves the right to amend or revoke this trust, in whole or in part, to withdraw property from it, and to make gifts from it at any time or times during the Settlor's lifetime.

B. On the death of the Settlor the trust created by this Declaration shall become irrevocable and not subject to amendment.

C. In this instrument, the terms "incompetent" and "disabled" shall refer to a physical or mental inability to carry out one's usual business affairs, whether or not such person is legally determined to be incompetent or in need of a Conservator. The Trustee, or a Successor Trustee, may rely upon a written declaration to determine the incompetence of the Settlor made by his daughter **[CHILD'S NAME]** if she has attained the age of 30. If she has not attained the age of the 30, then the declaration shall be made by, in order of priority, either 1) **[SUCCESSOR TRUSTEE 1]** or 2) **[SUCCESSOR TRUSTEE 2]**, sisters of the Settlor.

Any action taken by a Successor Trustee pursuant to such declaration shall be binding on all persons interested in the trust. No statement of incapacity from any physician shall be required to prove a change of Trustee as it is the Settlor's specific intention that physicians and courts not be involved in the determination of incapacity for any purpose. No third party shall incur any liability for relying on such declaration to prove a change of Trustee.

ARTICLE FOUR

During the life of the Settlor, the Trustee shall pay to or apply for the benefit of the Settlor at least annually all of the net income of the Trust Estate. If the Trustee considers the net income insufficient, the Trustee shall pay to the Settlor as much of the principal of the Trust Estate as is necessary in the Trustee's discretion for the Settlor's proper health, support, maintenance, comfort and welfare.

The Settlor wishes the Trustee, to the extent practical, to exercise discretion to enable the Settlor to live at home and in familiar circumstances if he wishes and is reasonably able to do so with nursing, household and other assistance even if the costs of being cared for at home may exceed the cost of care at a health-care institution, or the like.

ARTICLE FIVE

On the death of the Settlor, the Trustee, in the Trustee's discretion, shall pay out of the Trust Estate debts of the Settlor, and estate and inheritance taxes, including interest and penalties arising because of the Settlor's death; the last illness and funeral expenses of the Settlor, attorney's fees; and other costs incurred in administering the Settlor's Trust, probate estate, or unsupervised administration of the Settlor's assets. These payments shall be paid from the portion of the Trust Estate described in Article Six without charge against any beneficiary of the Trust Estate.

ARTICLE SIX

A. (1) Upon the death of the Settlor, [YOUR FULL NAME], the successor Trustee, after making payments provided in Article Five, shall retain twenty five percent (25%) of the Trust Estate in trust for the benefit of [FATHER'S NAME], father of the Settlor. The Trustee shall pay such sums from the income and principal of this trust share for the benefit of the Settlor's father as the Trustee deems appropriate. The beneficiary shall have no right to demand any distribution from this trust share and the existence of this trust share shall not be included as a resource of the beneficiary for the purposes of determining his eligibility based on financial need for any program or benefit. Upon the death of [FATHER'S NAME] the balance then remaining of this share shall be distributed as part of the residue of the Trust Estate.

The residue of the Trust Estate shall be distributed, free of trust, to [DAUGHTER'S NAME], daughter of the Settlor, by right of representation, subject to the provisions set forth in paragraph B herein below. If [DAUGHTER'S NAME] does not survive the Settlor and leaves no issue, then the residue of the Trust Estate shall be distributed to [BENEFICIARY 1] and [BENEFICIARY 2] by right of representation.

B. (1) If there are any beneficiaries, who are under the age of 30 at the time they become entitled to a share of the trust estate, the trustees shall pay to or apply for the benefit of all such beneficiaries, as much of the net income and principal of the trust as the trustee in the trustees' discretion considers necessary for the beneficiaries' proper support, health, maintenance, and education at an accredited academic institution, considering to the extent the trustee considers advisable any other income or resources known to the trustee for that beneficiary.

When the beneficiary has attained the age of 30, the trustees shall distribute the remaining assets free of trust to the beneficiary.

ARTICLE SEVEN

A. If the individual Trustee named in Article One, [YOUR FULL NAME], shall for any reason cease to act or be incompetent to act, then [DAUGHTER'S NAME] shall act as Trustee provided she has attained the age of 30. If she has not attained the age of 30, then the successor Trustee shall be, in order of priority, 1) [SUCCESSOR TRUSTEE 1] or 2) [SUCCESSOR TRUSTEE 2].

B. Any successor Trustee appointed as provided in this Declaration shall on appointment being made, immediately succeed to all title of the Trustee to the Trust Estate and to all powers, rights, discretions, obligations, and immunities of the Trustee under this Declaration with the same effect as though such successor were originally named as Trustee in this Declaration.

C. Any Trustee may resign without need of court approval by giving written notice to a successor Trustee who accepts the trust. A successor Trustee may be selected by a resigning Trustee if the Settlor has not provided for one in this declaration. Under no circumstances shall a corporate trustee serve as trustee of any trust created under this instrument. A Trustee shall not be removed as a Trustee based on a conflict of interest only because they are also a beneficiary.

D. No bond shall be required of any person named in this instrument as Trustee, or of any person appointed as the Trustee in the manner specified here, for the faithful performance of his or her duties as Trustee.

ARTICLE EIGHT

In order to carry out the provisions of the Trusts created by this instrument, the Trustee shall have these powers in addition to those now or hereafter conferred by the law:

(a) The Trustee may, in the Trustee's discretion, invest and reinvest trust funds in every kind of property (real, personal, or mixed) and every kind of investment, specifically including, but not limited to, corporate obligations of every kind; preferred or common stocks; shares of investment trusts, investment companies, and mutual funds; life insurance policies; notes, real estate, bonds, debentures, mortgages, deeds of trust, mortgage participations, market funds and index funds appropriate under the then prevailing circumstances (specifically including, but not limited to, the factors set out in probate Code section 16047(c)):

1. General economic conditions.
2. The possible effect of inflation or deflation.
3. The expected tax consequences of investment decisions or strategies
4. The role that teach investment or course of action plays within the overall trust portfolio.
5. The expected total return from income and the appreciation of capital.
6. Other resources of the beneficiaries known to the Trustee as determined from information provided by the beneficiaries.
7. Needs for liquidity, regularity of income, and preservation or appreciation of capital.
8. An asset's special relationship or special value, if any, to the purposes of the trust or to one or more of the beneficiaries.

In so doing, the Trustee shall exercise care, skill, and caution to attain the Settlor's goals under this instrument.

The Trustee shall consider individual investments as part of an overall investment strategy having risk and return objectives reasonably suited to the purposes of the trust. The Trustee's investments may include stock in any entity owned by the Trustee or membership in any limited liability company or limited liability partnership of which the Trustee is a member or partner.

The Trustee shall also have the power to establish and maintain margin accounts and to buy or sell options but only when the Settlor is acting as Trustee.

(b) To continue to hold any property and to operate at the risk of the Trust Estate any business that the Trustee receives or acquires under the Trust as long as the Trustee deems advisable.

(c) To have all the rights, powers, and privileges of an owner with respect to the securities held in trust, including, but not limited to, the powers to vote, give proxies, and pay assessments; to participate in voting trusts, pooling agreements, foreclosures, reorganizations, consolidations, mergers, and liquidations, and incident to such participation to deposit securities with and transfer title to any protective or other committee on such terms as the Trustee may deem advisable; and to exercise or sell stock subscription or conversion rights.

(d) To hold securities or other property in the Trustee's name as Trustee under this Trust.

(e) To manage, control, grant options on, sell (for cash or on deferred payments), convey, exchange, divide, improve, and repair Trust property.

(f) To rent and or lease Trust property for terms within or beyond the term of the Trust for any purpose, including exploration for and removal of gas, oil, and other minerals; and to enter into community oil leases, pooling, and unitization agreements.

(g) To lend money to the probate estate of the Settlor, provided that any such loan shall be adequately secured and shall bear a reasonable rate of interest.

(h) To purchase property at its fair market value as determined by the Trustee in the Trustee's discretion, from the probate estate of the Settlor.

(i) To loan or advance the Trustee's own funds to the Trust for any Trust purpose, with interest at current rates; to receive security for such loans in the form of a mortgage, pledge, deed of trust, or other encumbrance of any assets of the Trust; to purchase assets of the Trust at their fair market value as determined by an independent appraisal.

(j) The Trustee shall have the power to release or to restrict the scope of any power that he or she may hold in connection with the Trust created under this instrument, whether said power is expressly granted in this instrument or implied by law.

(k) To take any action and to make any election, in the Trustee's discretion, to minimize the tax liabilities of this Trust and its beneficiaries, and it shall have the power to allocate the benefits among the various beneficiaries, and the Trustee shall have the power to make adjustments in the rights of any beneficiaries, or between the income and principal accounts, to compensate for the consequences of any tax election or any investment or administrative decision that the Trustee believes has had the effect of directly or indirectly preferring one beneficiary or group of beneficiaries over others.

(l) To borrow money, and to encumber Trust property by mortgage, deed of trust, pledge, or otherwise of the debts of the Trust or the joint debts of the Trust and a co-owner of Trust property.

(m) To commence or defend, at the expense of the Trust, such litigation with respect to the Trust or any property of the Trust Estate as the Trustee may deem advisable, and to compromise or otherwise adjust any claims or litigation against or in favor of the Trust.

(n) To carry insurance of such kinds and in such amounts as the Trustee deems advisable, at the expense of the Trust, to protect the Trust Estate and the Trustee personally against any hazard.

(o) To withhold from distribution, in the Trustee's discretion, at the time for distribution of any property in this Trust, without the payment of interest, all or any part of the property, as long as the Trustee shall determine, in the Trustee's discretion, that such property may be subject to conflicting claims, to tax deficiencies, or to liabilities, contingent or otherwise properly incurred in the administration of the estate.

(p) To partition, allot, and distribute the Trust Estate, on any division or partial distribution or final distribution of the Trust Estate, in undivided interests or in kind, or partly in money and partly in kind, at valuations determined by the Trustee, and to sell such property as the Trustee may deem necessary to make division or distribution. In making any division or distribution of the Trust Estate, the Trustee shall be under no obligation to make a prorata division, or to distribute the same assets to beneficiaries similarly situated. The Trustee may, in the Trustee's discretion, make a nonproata division between Trusts or shares and nonprorata distributions to such beneficiaries, as long as the respective assets allocated to separate trusts or shares, or distributed to such beneficiaries, have equivalent or proportionate fair market value and income tax basis.

(q) Each Trustee shall have the power to employ any custodian, attorney, accountant, financial planner, investment advisor or any other agent to assist the Trustee in the administration of this Trust and to rely on the advice given by these agents.

(r) Subject to any limitations expressly set forth in this Declaration and the faithful performance of its fiduciary obligations, to do all such acts, take all such proceedings, and exercise all such rights and privileges as could be done, taken, or exercised by an absolute owner of the Trust property.

(s) The Trustee shall have the power to deal with governmental agencies. To make applications for, receive and administer Social Security, Medicare, Medicaid, Supplemental Security Income, In-Home Support Services, and any other benefits to which the Settlor or a beneficiary might be entitled.

(t) The Trustee shall have the power to make elections and direct distributions of principal and interest from the Settlor's retirement accounts, pension plans, or annuities that name the Trust as a primary or contingent beneficiary. Trust beneficiaries shall be treated as designated beneficiaries for the purpose of determining minimum distributions from an IRA based on the age of the oldest trust beneficiary. This power shall be construed as and is intended to be a valid power of attorney in which the Trustee may act as the agent of the Settlor for these purposes.

(u) The Trustee shall have the power to exercise any stock options held by the Settlor at the time of death.

(v) The Trustee shall be entitled to pay him- or herself reasonable compensation for services rendered to the Trust without prior court approval, not to exceed one percent per year of asset value.

ARTICLE NINE

A. The Trustee shall provide an accounting at the request of any current or remainder beneficiary if the Settlor is not acting as Trustee in which case accountings are waived.

B. The validity of this trust for real property shall be governed by the law of the state of its situs. The validity, construction, interpretation, and administration of this trust shall be governed by the law of the state of California regardless of its situs or the domicile of the Trustee with regard to all other matters.

C. In the event any beneficiary under this Trust shall, singly or in conjunction with any other person or persons, contest in any court the validity of this Trust or of the deceased Settlor's last Will or shall seek to obtain an adjudication in any proceeding in any court that this Trust or any of its provisions is invalid, then the right of that person to take any interest given to him or her by this Trust shall be determined as it would have been determined had the person predeceased the execution of this Declaration of Trust without surviving issue. The term contest shall include, but not be limited to, contests regarding the separate character of the property of this trust or the governing law provisions.

Executed at _____, _____ on _____, 20___.
              (City)   (State)   (Date)

_____
(Your signature)
[YOUR FULL NAME]

State of   )
County of   ) ss.

On_____, before me, _____, Notary Public, personally appeared **[YOUR FULL NAME]**, personally known to me or proved to me on the basis of satisfactory evidence to be the person whose name is subscribed to the within instrument and acknowledged to me that he executed the same in his authorized capacity, and that by his signature on the instrument the person or entity upon behalf of which he acted, executed the instrument. WITNESS my hand and official seal.

                                                      (Notary Seal)

_____
Signature of Notary

SAMPLE COUPLE REVOCABLE TRUST

[YOUR FULL NAME] and [SPOUSE'S FULL NAME] REVOCABLE TRUST

This declaration of trust is executed on _____, 20___, by [YOUR FULL NAME] and [SPOUSE'S FULL NAME] hereafter called "Settlors" or "Trustees" and sometimes wife and husband depending on the context. They hereby declare that they have set aside or transferred or will transfer property to themselves as Trustees and they will hold the property so transferred on the terms set forth in this declaration.

Article I (The Trust Estate)

TRUST ESTATE. The "Trust Estate" consists of the property transferred to the trust by the Settlors or their wills, as insurance proceeds or pension benefits, or (if acceptable to the Trustee) from any other person or source.

TRUST ESTATE IS COMMUNITY PROPERTY. All property listed in the trust and any property subsequently added to the Trust Estate by the Settlors is and shall remain the community property of the Settlors during their joint lifetime. Any power reserved to the Settlors to alter, amend, modify, or revoke this trust, in whole or in part, is held by the Settlors during their joint lifetimes in their capacity as managers of the community property, subject to all restrictions imposed by law on their management of the community property. If the trust is revoked, this community property shall be returned to the Settlors as their community property and not as the separate property of either Settlor.

Article II (Power to Revoke and Amend)

A. REVOCATION. During the Settlors' joint lifetime this trust may be revoked, in whole or in part, by an instrument in writing signed by both Settlors jointly or by either Settlor alone. On revocation, the Trustees shall deliver the Trust Estate or the revoked portion thereof to either or both of the Settlors, in either event as the community property of both Settlors.

B. AMENDMENT. During the Settlors' joint lifetime the terms of this trust may be amended, with respect to all or any part of the Trust Estate or terms, only by an instrument in writing signed by both Settlors. If neither Settlor is a Trustee, the instrument shall be delivered by a Settlor personally, by certified mail, or any other form of deliver requiring proof of receipt to the then acting Trustee.

C. DISABILITY OF SETTLOR(S). All of the Settlors' powers to revoke and amend are personal to them. The disability of one Settlor shall not prevent exercise by the other Settlor of his or her power of revocation for the purpose of holding some or all of the property as community property outside the Trust Estate.

D. DEATH OF SETTLORS. Upon the death of the first Settlor to die, the Surviving Settlor may revoke or amend the trust by an instrument in writing signed by the Surviving Settlor. If the Settlor is not acting as Trustee, the amendment shall be delivered by the Settlor personally, by certified mail, or any other form of deliver requiring proof of receipt to the then acting Trustee. If any portion of the trust is revoked, the Trustees shall be entitled to retain assets required for the payment of liabilities properly incurred in administering the trust, unless indemnified by a Settlor against loss or expense.

On the death of the second Settlor to die the trust created by this Declaration shall become irrevocable and not subject to amendment.

Article III (Distribution of Income and Principal During Settlors' Joint Lifetime)

A. As long as both Settlors are alive, the Trustees shall pay to either or both of the Settlors or apply for their benefit and care, in at least annual installments, the net income of the trust and also as much of the principal of the Trust Estate as the Trustees deem appropriate for the Settlors' support, comfort, health, care and general welfare.

B. A SETTLOR'S "CARE." The term "care" as used throughout this declaration with regard to the

Settlors shall include maintaining them during their lifetime in their regular residences, or elsewhere as may be appropriate, despite a need for extensive medical or personal care at a cost that may exceed the cost of care at a home for the elderly, a health-care institution, or the like. The Settlors wish the Trustee, to the extent practical, to exercise discretion under these provisions to enable them to live at home and in familiar circumstances if they wish and are reasonably able to do so with nursing, household and other assistance.

C. The Settlors, acting jointly, may at any time direct the trustees to pay single sums or periodic payments out of the trust estate to any other person or organization.

Article IV (Determination of Incapacity or Disability)

In this instrument, the terms "incompetent" and "disabled" shall refer to a physical or mental inability to carry out one's usual business affairs, whether or not such person is legally determined to be incompetent or in need of a Conservator. The Trustee, or a Successor Trustee, may rely upon a written declaration made by either Settlor as to the other Settlor as to the incompetence or disability of the Settlor. If a Settlor is not available to make a determination of incapacity, then the declaration shall be made by, in order of priority, 1) [OPTION 1] or 2) [OPTION 2]. Any action taken by such a Successor Trustee pursuant to such declaration shall be binding on all persons interested in the trust. No statement of incapacity from any physician shall be required to prove a change of Trustee as it is the Settlors' specific intention that physicians and courts not be involved in the determination of incapacity for any purpose. No third party shall incur any liability for relying on such declaration to prove a change of Trustee.

Article V (Payments Upon Death of First Settlor to Die)

A. On the death of the first Settlor to die the Trust Estate, including all of the community property of the Settlors that is received by the Trustees from insurance, pension plans and other sources as community property upon or by reason of the death of the Settlor, shall be retained in trust for the benefit of the Surviving Settlor. The Trustee shall pay to the surviving Settlor or apply for their benefit and care, in at least annual installments, the net income of the trust and also as much of the principal of the Trust Estate as the Trustees deem appropriate for the Settlor's support, comfort, health, care and general welfare.

Article VI (Distribution of the Trust on Surviving Settlor's Death)

On the death of the Surviving Settlor, the Trust Estate shall then be administered and distributed by the Trustees as follows:

A. On the surviving spouse's death, the Trustee, in the Trustee's discretion, may pay out of the Trust Estate the deceased spouse's debts outstanding at the time of his or her death and not barred by the statute of limitations, or any other provision of law, the federal or state estate and inheritance taxes, including interest and penalties, the last illness and funeral expenses of the deceased spouse, attorneys' fees, and other costs incurred in administering the deceased spouse's probate estate. Any payments for estate or inheritance taxes shall be charged to the Trust Estate without apportionment or charge against any beneficiary of the Trust Estate. Payments for last illness, funeral, and other administration costs shall be charged to the Trust Estate.

The Trustee shall distribute the residue of the Trust Estate to the Settlors' children, namely [CHILD 1], [CHILD 2], and [CHILD 3] by right of representation. If the Settlors are not survived by issue, then the residue of the Trust Estate shall be distributed, free of trust, to the American Red Cross, a tax exempt organization.

B. (1) If there are any beneficiaries, who are under the age of 30 at the time they become entitled to a share of the trust estate, the trustees shall pay to or apply for the benefit of all such beneficiaries, as much of the net income and principal of the trust as the trustee in the trustees' discretion considers necessary for the beneficiaries' proper support, health, maintenance, and education at an accredited academic institution, considering to the extent the trustee considers advisable any other income or resources known to the trustee for that beneficiary.

When the beneficiary has attained the age of 30, the trustees shall distribute the remaining assets free of trust to the beneficiary.

Article VII (The Trustees and Their Powers)

A. Except as otherwise expressly provided, all references and grants of powers to the Trustee in this declaration of trust apply not only to the original Trustee but also to any substitute or successor Trustee or Trustees.

B. Trustees The Settlors shall serve as Co-Trustees for each trust created under this declaration during their joint lifetime. Upon the death or incapacity of either Settlor the remaining Settlor shall become sole Trustee. Upon the death or incapacity of both Settlors then there shall be one Trustee who shall be, in order of priority, either 1) [**TRUSTEE 1**], brother of husband or 2) [**TRUSTEE 2**].

(1) RESIGNATION. A Trustee may resign at any time by an instrument in writing delivered personally, by certified mail, or other form of deliver requiring proof of receipt, to either or both of the Settlors during their joint lifetime or to a successor Trustee who may be appointed by the resigning Trustee and who accepts the appointment. A resigning Trustee shall promptly deliver the Trust Estate to the remaining or new Trustee, accompanied by an accounting that is appropriate to the circumstances. Under no circumstances, however, shall a corporate Trustee be appointed as Trustee for any trust created under this declaration.

(2) SETTLORS AS TRUSTEES. As long as both Settlors are acting in their capacity as Trustees, the Trustees shall have the authority to open any type of accounts offered by conventional banking or brokerage institutions in the name of the trust. These accounts may require the signature of only one Trustee in order to facilitate the daily banking and trading activities of the trust. The powers of the Trustees remain subject to all other provisions of the trust.

C. POWERS OF THE TRUSTEES. In order to carry out the provisions of the Trusts created by this instrument, the Trustee shall have these powers in addition to those now or hereafter conferred by the law:

(1) To invest and reinvest all or any part of the Trust Estate in conventional bank accounts, including any account offered by conventional bank, precious metals, oil and gas investments, money market funds, such common or preferred stocks, shares of investment trusts or investment companies, bonds, debentures, mortgages, deeds of trust, mortgage participations, notes, real estate, or other property as the Trustee, in the Trustee's discretion, may select; and the Trustee may continue to hold in the form in which received (or the form to which changed by reorganization, split-up, stock dividend, or to like occurrence) any securities or other property the Trustee may at any time acquire under this Trust, it being the Settlor's express desire and intention that the Trustee shall have full power to invest and reinvest the Trust funds without being restricted to forms of investment that the Trustee may otherwise be permitted to make by law; and the investments need not be diversified.

(2) To continue to hold any property including any shares of the Trustee's own stock and to operate at the risk of the Trust Estate any business that the Trustee receives or acquires under the Trust as long as the Trustee deems advisable.

(3) To have all the rights, powers, and privileges of an owner with respect to the securities held in trust, including, but not limited to, the powers to vote, give proxies, and pay assessments; to participate in voting trusts, pooling agreements, foreclosures, reorganizations, consolidations, mergers, and liquidations, and incident to such participation to deposit securities with and transfer title to any protective or other committee on such terms as the Trustee may deem advisable; and to exercise or sell stock subscription or conversion rights.

(4) To hold securities or other property in the Trustee's name as Trustee under this Trust.

(5) To manage, control, grant options on, sell (for cash or on deferred payments), convey, exchange, partition, divide, improve, and repair Trust property.

(6) To rent and or lease Trust property for terms within or beyond the term of the Trust for any purpose, including exploration for and removal of gas, oil, and other minerals; and to enter into community oil leases, pooling, and unitization agreements.

(7) To lend money to the probate estate of the Settlor, provided that any such loan shall be adequately secured and shall bear a reasonable rate of interest.

(8) To purchase property at its fair market value as determined by the Trustee in the Trustee's discretion, from the probate estate of the Settlor.

(9) To loan or advance the Trustee's own funds to the Trust for any Trust purpose, with interest at current rates; to receive security for such loans in the form of a mortgage, pledge, deed of trust, or other encumbrance of any assets of the Trust; to purchase assets of the Trust at their fair market value as determined by an independent appraisal.

(10) The Trustee shall have the power to release or to restrict the scope of any power that he or she may hold in connection with the Trust created under this instrument, whether said power is expressly granted in this instrument or implied by law. The Trustee shall exercise this power in a written instrument specifying the powers to by released or restricted and the nature of any such restriction.

(11) To take any action and to make any election, in the Trustee's discretion, to minimize the tax liabilities of this Trust and its beneficiaries, and it shall have the power to allocate the benefits among the various beneficiaries, and the Trustee shall have the power to make adjustments in the rights of any beneficiaries, or between the income and principal accounts, to compensate for the consequences of any tax election or any investment or administrative decision that the Trustee believes has had the effect of directly or indirectly preferring one beneficiary or group of beneficiaries over others.

(12) To borrow money, and to encumber Trust property by mortgage, deed of trust, pledge, or otherwise of the debts of the Trust or the joint debts of the Trust and a co-owner of Trust property.

(13) To commence or defend, at the expense of the Trust, such litigation with respect to the Trust or any property of the Trust Estate as the Trustee may deem advisable, and to compromise or otherwise adjust any claims or litigation against or in favor of the Trust.

(14) To carry insurance of such kinds and in such amounts as the Trustee deems advisable, at the expense of the Trust, to protect the Trust Estate and the Trustee personally against any hazard.

(15) To withhold from distribution, in the Trustee's discretion, at the time for distribution of any property in this Trust, without the payment of interest, all or any part of the property, as long as the Trustee shall determine, in the Trustee's discretion, that such property may be subject to conflicting claims, to tax deficiencies, or to liabilities, contingent or otherwise properly incurred in the administration of the estate.

(16) To purchase bonds, and to pay such premiums in connection with the purchase as the Trustee, in the Trustee's discretion, deems advisable, provided, however, that each premium shall be repaid periodically to principal out of the interest on the bond in such reasonable manner as the Trustee shall determine and, to the extent necessary, out of the proceeds on the sale or other disposition of the bond.

(17) To purchase bonds at such discount as the Trustee, in the Trustee' discretion, deems advisable, provided, however, that each discount shall be accumulated periodically as interest in such reasonable manner as the Trustee shall determine and to the extent necessary paid out of the proceeds on the sale or other disposition of the bond or out of principal.

(18) To partition, allot, and distribute the Trust Estate, on any division or partial distribution or final distribution of the Trust Estate, in undivided interests or in kind, or partly in money and partly in kind, at valuations determined by the Trustee, and to sell such property as the Trustee may deem necessary to make division or distribution. In making any division or partial or final distribution of the Trust Estate, the Trustee shall be under no obligation to make a prorata division, or to distribute the same assets to beneficiaries similarly situated; but rather, the Trustee may, in the Trustee's discretion, make a nonprorata division between Trusts or shares and nonprorata distributions to such beneficiaries, as long as the respective assets allocated to separate trusts or shares, or distributed to such beneficiaries, have equivalent or proportionate fair market value an income tax bases.

(19) Each Trustee shall have the power to employ any attorney, accountant, financial planner, investment advisor or any other agent or agents to assist the Trustee in the administration of this Trust and to rely on the advice given by these agents.

(20) The Trustee shall have the power to deal with governmental agencies. To make applications for, receive and administer any of the following benefits: Social Security, Medicare, Medicaid, Supplemental Security Income, In-Home Support Services, and any other government resources and community support services available to the elderly.

(21) The Trustee shall have the power to make elections and direct distributions from either Settlors' retirement accounts, pension plans or annuities that name the Trust as a primary or contingent beneficiary. Trust beneficiaries shall be treated as designated beneficiaries for the purpose of determining minimum distributions from an IRA based on the age of the oldest trust beneficiary. This power shall be construed as and is intended to be a valid power of attorney in which the Trustee may act as the agent of either Settlor for these purposes.

(22) The Trustee shall be entitled to pay him or her self reasonable compensation for services rendered to the Trust without need of prior court approval so long as such compensation does not exceed one percent per year of the asset value of the Trust.

Article VIII (General Provisions)

A. The construction of the provisions of this declaration and its administration shall be governed by the internal laws of the State of California and not conflict of laws rules regardless of the situs of the Trust or the domicile of the Trustees.

B. The Settlors waive the annual accounting requirements for any trust created under this declaration as found in California Probate Code Section 16062 unless someone other than a Settlor is acting as a Trustee in which case accountings shall be provided at the request of any current or remainder beneficiary.

C. A contestant shall be considered to have predeceased both Settlors without surviving issue. In this instrument, "contestant" means any person other than the Settlors who, directly or indirectly, voluntarily participates in any proceeding or action which seeks to void or set aside any provision of this trust, any provision of either Settlor's will; or any amendment of this instrument or codicil of either Settlor's will. The term contest shall include but not be limited to contests regarding the character of trust property or governing law provisions.

This trust shall be known as the [YOUR FULL NAME] and [SPOUSE'S FULL NAME] Revocable Trust.

Executed at _____ _____ on _____, 20___.
            (City)   (State)   (Date)

_____   _____
(Your signature)   (Spouse's signature)
[YOUR FULL NAME]   **[SPOUSE'S FULL NAME]**

State of   )
County of   ) ss

On _____, 20___ before me, _____, Notary Public, personally appeared **[YOUR FULL NAME]** and **[SPOUSE'S FULL NAME]** personally known to me or proved to me on the basis of satisfactory evidence to be the person(s) whose names are subscribed to the within instrument and acknowledged to me that they executed the same in their authorized capacity, and that by their signatures on the instrument the persons or the entity upon behalf of which the persons acted, executed the instrument. WITNESS my hand and official seal.

(Notary Seal)

_____
Signature of Notary

HOW TO FUND THE REVOCABLE TRUST— SINGLE

In order to avoid probate, assets must be transferred into the trust. All major assets such as real estate, stocks, savings accounts, bonds, and limited partnerships should be in the trust. This should be done as soon as is practical after the trust is signed.

The terms "Revocable Living Trust" and "Revocable Trust" are used interchangeably in the Protection Portfolio materials. The phrase "Revocable Trust" is the recognized legal description and should be used in the title of your trust documents.

The legal title of your assets is changed—instead of holding title as [YOUR FULL NAME], the new title will be: [YOUR FULL NAME] as Trustee of the [YOUR FULL NAME] REVOCABLE TRUST.

The date you signed the trust will be important and can be given to further identify the trust. This date is often requested by financial institutions when you fill out the funding documents for your trust. It is also known as the UDT (Under Declaration of Trust Dated). Even if you restate your trust at a later date, the original date stated is the legal date of the trust. The tax ID number for the trust can be your Social Security number.

You can be identified as the Trustor/Grantor/Settlor of the trust and you are also the Trustee.

SAFE-DEPOSIT BOX
Many people want to keep their original trust and wills in a safe-deposit box in case of fire. The title to the box should be [YOUR FULL NAME] as Trustee of the [YOUR FULL NAME] REVOCABLE TRUST.

REAL PROPERTY
The only way to change title to real property is by recording a deed in the office of the County Recorder where the property is located. When you purchase new property, take title as indicated above and the property will be in the trust from the beginning.

It is important to consult a local real estate lawyer or title company to ensure that the deeds are created specifically for your location. Different states and counties within the same state have specific requirements that must appear in the deed to preserve homestead exemptions and property tax rates. The cost is usually less than $125 per deed.

BANK ACCOUNTS, PARTNERSHIPS, BROKERAGE ACCOUNTS, ETC.
The title to all such accounts should be [YOUR FULL NAME] as Trustee of the [YOUR FULL NAME] REVOCABLE TRUST.

PROMISSORY NOTES

If you hold a promissory note signed by someone in your favor, then the note can be assigned to the trust by endorsing the back of the note as follows:

I assign my interest in the within promissory note to [YOUR FULL NAME] as Trustee of the [YOUR FULL NAME] REVOCABLE TRUST.

Signature _____ Dated: _____

(Date of assignment)

You should advise the payor of the note to make future payments to you in your name as Trustee. Secured notes should be assigned by a formal assignment that is recorded in the same manner as the original trust deed.

PENSION PLANS, IRA, LIFE INSURANCE, ANNUITIES

These investments make direct payments to the named beneficiary, so they avoid probate anyway. To name or change beneficiaries, request designation of beneficiary forms from the insurance company, your company pension plan, or the company administering your IRA or pension plan.

HOW TO FUND THE REVOCABLE TRUST—MARRIED

In order to avoid probate, assets must be transferred into the trust. All major assets such as real estate, stocks, savings accounts, bonds, and limited partnerships should be in the trust. This should be done as soon as is practical after the trust is signed.

The terms "Revocable Living Trust" and "Revocable Trust" are used interchangeably in the Protection Portfolio materials. The phrase "Revocable Trust" is the recognized legal description and should be used in the title of your trust documents.

The legal title of your assets is changed—instead of holding title as [YOUR FULL NAME] and [YOUR SPOUSE'S FULL NAME], the new title will be: [YOUR FULL NAME] and [YOUR SPOUSE'S FULL NAME] as Trustees of the [YOUR FULL NAME] and [YOUR SPOUSE'S FULL NAME] REVOCABLE TRUST.

The date you signed the trust will be important and can be given to further identify the trust. This date is often requested by financial institutions when you fill out the funding documents for your trust. It is also known as the UDT (Under Declaration of Trust Dated). Even if you restate your trust at a later date, the original date stated is the legal date of the trust. The tax ID number for the trust can be either one of your Social Security numbers.

You can be identified as the Trustors/Grantors/Settlors of the trust and you are also the Trustees.

SAFE-DEPOSIT BOX
Many people want to keep their original trust and wills in a safe-deposit box in case of fire. The title to the box should be [YOUR FULL NAME] and [YOUR SPOUSE'S FULL NAME] as Trustees of the [YOUR FULL NAME] and [YOUR SPOUSE'S FULL NAME] REVOCABLE TRUST.

REAL PROPERTY
The only way to change title to real property is by recording a deed in the office of the County Recorder where the property is located. When you purchase new property, take title as indicated above and the property will be in the trust from the beginning.

It is important to consult a local real estate lawyer or title company to ensure that the deeds are created specifically for your location. Different states and counties within the same state have specific requirements that must appear in the deed to preserve homestead exemptions and property tax rates. The cost is usually less than $125 per deed.

BANK ACCOUNTS, PARTNERSHIPS, BROKERAGE ACCOUNTS, ETC.
The title to all such accounts should be [YOUR FULL NAME] and [YOUR SPOUSE'S FULL NAME] as Trustees of the [YOUR FULL NAME] and [YOUR SPOUSE'S FULL NAME] REVOCABLE TRUST.

PROMISSORY NOTES
If you hold a promissory note signed by someone in your favor, then the note can be assigned to the trust by endorsing the back of the note as follows:

I (We) assign my (our) interest in the within promissory note to [YOUR FULL NAME] and [YOUR SPOUSE'S FULL NAME] as Trustees of the [YOUR FULL NAME] and [YOUR SPOUSE'S FULL NAME] REVOCABLE TRUST.

Signature _____ Dated: _____
(Date of assignment)

Signature _____ Dated: _____
(Date of assignment)

You should advise the payor of the note to make future payments to you in your names as Trustees. Secured notes should be assigned by a formal assignment that is recorded in the same manner as the original trust deed.

PENSION PLANS, IRA, LIFE INSURANCE, ANNUITIES
These investments make direct payments to the named beneficiary, so they avoid probate anyway. However, you want to be sure the funds come into the trust if your spouse predeceases you. Therefore, name your spouse as the primary beneficiary and the trust as the contingent beneficiary. To name or change beneficiaries, request designation of beneficiary forms from the insurance company, your company pension plan, or the company administering your IRA or pension plan.

FUNDING YOUR TRUST—MUTUAL FUNDS CHANGE OF OWNERSHIP LETTER

_____

_____

_____

Mutual Fund Account # _____

To whom it may concern:

I recently created the [YOUR FULL NAME] **Revocable Trust** dated _____, 20___. I would like to change the title of my account to [YOUR FULL NAME] as trustee of the [YOUR FULL NAME] **Revocable Trust.**

I request that this change be made effective immediately to protect my assets from the cost of probate. If you have any questions regarding this change, please contact me at:

(__) _____ *(phone)*

_____ *(address)*

_____

_____ *(SS #)*

Medallion Signatures Guarantee

_____
(Name of Bank or Broker)

By_____
(Authorized Signature)

_____

_____

_____
(Branch Address)

Please return this letter in the self-addressed stamped envelope and indicate
(1) Instruction to re-register account received_____
(2) New registration completed_____
(3) Forms enclosed to complete change of registration request _____

FUNDING YOUR TRUST—ASSIGNMENT OF BUSINESS INTEREST

This assignment is effective _____, 20___ by and between [YOUR FULL NAME] and [YOUR FULL NAME] as trustee of the [YOUR FULL NAME] REVOCABLE TRUST executed _____, 20___.

[YOUR FULL NAME] assigns and transfers to the trustees all the right, title, and interest in and to all the tangible personal property owned by the business known as [BUSINESS NAME] located at [ADDRESS, [CITY], [STATE], USA. The term tangible personal property refers, without limitation, to such items as furniture, furnishings, computers, business machines and other tangible personal property normally kept at the business. I also assigns all of the goodwill of the business, the lease for the business location, all accounts receivables and accounts payable of the business and any other interest associated in any way with [BUSINESS NAME].

_____
(Your signature)

[YOUR FULL NAME]

FUNDING YOUR TRUST—ASSIGNMENT OF RIGHT TO EXERCISE STOCK OPTION PLAN AFTER DEATH OF SETTLOR

THIS ASSIGNMENT is made by [YOUR FULL NAME], hereafter referred to as the "Assignor."

1. The Assignor currently holds the right to exercise an option to purchase the stock of [CORPORATION NAME], under the terms of a stock option agreement dated _____. [A copy of the agreement is attached to this instrument.]

2. The Assignor created the [YOUR FULL NAME] REVOCABLE TRUST on _____ 20___. The Assignor is currently serving as trustee of that trust. Under the terms of that trust, the Assignor has retained all beneficial interest in any real or personal property thereafter transferred to that trust.

3. The Assignor hereby assigns to the successor trustee of the [YOUR FULL NAME] REVOCABLE TRUST the right to exercise the above-described stock option after Assignor's death or disability. This assignment is effective immediately.

4. This assignment is accepted by [YOUR FULL NAME], trustee of the [YOUR FULL NAME] REVOCABLE TRUST dated 20___ on behalf of all successor trustees of that trust, and shall be exercisable by any trustee then serving.

IN WITNESS WHEREOF, the parties have executed this Assignment on _____ 20___.

(month, day)

ASSIGNOR: ASSIGNEE:

_____   _____
(Your signature)   *(Your signature)*
[YOUR FULL NAME]   [YOUR FULL NAME], Trustee

State of _____)
County of _____) ss.

On _____ 20___ before me, _____, Notary Public, personally appeared _____ personally known to me or proved to me on the basis of satisfactory evidence to be the person(s) whose names are subscribed to the within instrument and acknowledged to me that they executed the same in their authorized capacity, and that by their signatures on the instrument the persons or the entity upon behalf of which the persons acted, executed the instrument, WITNESS my hand and official seal.

(Notary Seal)

_____
Signature of Notary

FUNDING YOUR TRUST—BANK AND CREDIT UNION INSTRUCTION LETTER

RE:

Checking Account # _____
Savings Account # _____
Safe-Deposit Box _____

To whom it may concern:

I recently created the [YOUR FULL NAME] **Revocable Trust,** dated _____, 20___.
I would like to change the title of my account to [YOUR FULLNAME] as trustee of the [YOUR FULL NAME] **Revocable Trust,** dated _____, 20___.

If any additional forms are necessary, please forward them to me, [YOUR FULL NAME], at [ADDRESS], [CITY], [STATE], [ZIP]. You may also fax them to [FAX NUMBER]. Thank you for your cooperation.

Best regards,

_____
(Your signature)
[YOUR FULL NAME]

SSN #_____

Please return this letter in the self-addressed stamped envelope and indicate:

(1) Instruction to re-register account received _____
(2) New registration completed _____
(3) Forms enclosed to complete change of registration request _____

FUNDING YOUR TRUST—ASSIGNMENT OF LIMITED PARTNERSHIP INTEREST

PAGE ONE OF THREE
Assignment 1a

_____
_____

_____

Dear General Partner:

Enclosed please find an assignment of the interest of [YOUR FULL NAME] in the [PARTNER-SHIP NAME] Limited Partnership to the [YOUR FULL NAME] revocable trust. This trust has been created to avoid probate of the estate and provide for management in the case of disability, and is dated _____, 20___.

Please keep the original assignment with the partnership records and return your signed consent to me in the enclosed self-addressed stamped envelope.

Thank you!

FUNDING YOUR TRUST—ASSIGNMENT OF LIMITED PARTNERSHIP INTEREST
PAGE TWO OF THREE
Assignment 1b

Assignment of [PARTNERSHIP NAME] Limited Partnership Interest

For no consideration, [YOUR FULL NAME], hereby assigns all rights, title, and interest in and to the [PARTNERSHIP NAME] **Limited Partnership** to [YOUR FULL NAME] as trustee of the [YOUR FULL NAME] **Revocable Trust,** dated _____, 20___. This assignment shall be effective as of the date of this instrument. Hereafter, the trustee of the [YOUR FULL NAME] **Revocable Trust,** _____, 20___ shall have the same rights under the [PARTNERSHIP NAME] **Limited Partnership** agreement as the assignor.

Executed at _____, on _____, 20___.
         (City, State)   *(Date)*

_____
(Your signature)
[YOUR FULL NAME]

FUNDING YOUR TRUST—ASSIGNMENT OF LIMITED PARTNERSHIP INTEREST

PAGE THREE OF THREE

Assignment 1c

Consent to Assignment

The undersigned general partners of the [PARTNERSHIP NAME] Limited Partnership consent to the foregoing assignment, and approve the admission of the trustee of the [YOUR FULL NAME] **Revocable Trust** _____, 20___ to the partnership as a substituted limited partner, subject to all terms and conditions of the [PARTNERSHIP NAME] Limited Partnership agreement.

Executed at _____, on _____, 20___.
             (City, State)   *(Date)*

By _____
    (General Partner's signature)

FUNDING YOUR TRUST—AMENDMENT TO THE [COMPANY NAME] LLC

The operating agreement dated _____ governing the relationship among Members of the [COMPANY NAME], LLC, is hereby amended to reflect the assignment of **[YOUR FULL NAME]** of his/her interest in the company to **[YOUR FULL NAME]** as Trustee of the **[YOUR FULL NAME]** Revocable Trust dated _____, 20___.

The undersigned, being all the members of the company, hereby approve and consent to the assignment.

Therefore, the members of [COMPANY NAME], LLC, effective _____, 20___ are as follows:

Name   **Percentage Interest**

1. _____   65%   _____
   [YOUR FULL NAME]   *(Your signature)*
   as Trustee of the
   [YOUR FULL NAME]
   REVOCABLE TRUST

2. _____   15%   _____
   JOHN DOE   *(Signature)*

3. _____   10%   _____
   JANE DOE   *(Signature)*

4. _____   10%   _____
   JOE SMITH   *(Signature)*

FUNDING YOUR TRUST—IRA BENEFICIARY DESIGNATION FORM—SINGLE

NAME OF COMPANY: [COMPANY]
ACCOUNT NO: [IRA ACCOUNT NUMBER]
PARTICIPANT NAME: [YOUR FULL NAME]
PARTICIPANT SOCIAL SECURITY #: [000-00-0000]

PRIMARY BENEFICIARY

Name: [YOUR FULL NAME] Revocable Trust
Address: [ADDRESS] Date of Trust [DATE]   Shares 100 (%)
City: [CITY]   State: [STATE]   Zip Code:[ZIP]
Relationship: Family Trust   Social Security #: [000-00-0000]

_____   _____
SIGNATURE OF PARTICIPANT   DATE

State of   )
County of   )
On _____, 20___, before me, _____, Notary Public, personally
appeared _____ personally known to me or proved to me on the basis of satisfactory evidence to be the person(s) whose names are subscribed to the within instrument and acknowledged to me that
they executed the same in their authorized capacity, and that by their signatures on the instrument, the persons
or the entity upon behalf of which the persons acted, executed the instrument. WITNESS my hand and
official seal.

(Notary Seal)

_____
Signature of Notary

FUNDING YOUR TRUST—IRA BENEFICIARY DESIGNATION FORM—MARRIED

NAME OF COMPANY: [COMPANY]
ACCOUNT NO: [IRA ACCOUNT NUMBER]
PARTICIPANT NAME: [YOUR FULL NAME]
PARTICIPANT SOCIAL SECURITY #: [000-00-0000]

PRIMARY BENEFICIARY

Name: [SPOUSE'S NAME]
Address: [ADDRESS] Shares 100 (%)
City: [CITY]   State: [STATE]   Zip Code: [ZIP]
Relationship: Spouse   Social Security #: [000-00-0000]

CONTINGENT BENEFICIARY

Name: [YOUR FULL NAME] and [SPOUSE'S FULL NAME] Revocable Trust
Address: [ADDRESS] Date of Trust: [00-00-0000] Share: 100 (%)
City: [CITY]   State: [STATE]   Zip Code: [ZIP]
Relationship: Family Trust   Social Security#:   [000-00-0000]

_____   _____
SIGNATURE OF PARTICIPANT   DATE

State of   )
County of   )
On _____, 20___, before me, _____, Notary Public, personally
appeared _____ personally known to me or proved to me on the basis of
satisfactory evidence to be the person(s) whose names are subscribed to the within instrument and acknowledged to me that they executed the same in their authorized capacity, and that by their signatures on the
instrument, the persons or the entity upon behalf of which the persons acted, executed the instrument.
WITNESS my hand and official seal.

(Notary Seal)

_____
Signature of Notary

FINAL INSTRUCTIONS

To prepare for your death carefully is a supreme act of love toward those you will one day leave behind. It can greatly help your survivors emotionally, because having to deal with practical chaos after a loss makes the loss itself more painful and frightening. It can also help them financially, because careful estate planning may save them thousands of dollars in probate fees, estate taxes, and attorney's fees.

By having a will and a trust, you have helped to ensure that your family members will be taken care of financially. Now take the time to prepare your final instructions so that you can also help protect them emotionally as well.

Final Instructions Form

Please review the **"Final Instructions"** form on the next page. You can also find a copy of "Final Instructions" on your Protection Portfolio forms CD-ROM. Make sure that you fill out the form and place a copy in your Protection Portfolio so that your family will be aware of your last wishes.

Claiming Benefits

Chances are good that your spouse or life partner had a number of policies or accounts with benefits that you may be eligible for. Please check these thoroughly, following the instructions below.

Social Security Benefits

If the deceased had paid into Social Security for at least 40 quarters, two types of benefits are possible. You can apply for either one. You can apply by telephone or at any Social Security office:

1. Death benefit. A benefit of $255 for burial expenses is available to eligible spouses or dependent children. The survivor can complete the necessary form at a local Social Security office, or your funeral director may complete the application and apply the payment directly to the funeral bill.

2. Survivor's benefits. A variety of benefits is available, depending on the age and relationship you had with the deceased. You may be eligible for benefits if you match any of these descriptions:

- You are a spouse, age 60 or older
- You are a disabled surviving spouse, age 50 or older
- You are a spouse under 60 who cares for dependent children under 16 or for disabled children
- You are a child of the deceased under the age of 18 or who is disabled
- If you are not already receiving Social Security benefits at the time of your loved one's death, here are some other points to keep in mind:
- Apply promptly for survivor's benefits. In some cases, benefits may not be retroactive.
- Try to have the necessary information close at hand, but don't panic if you don't have it. Social Security will ask for specific information and documents in order to process your application. It will be helpful if you have it when you apply, but don't delay applying if you don't have everything. You will need either original documents or copies certified by the agency that issued them.

These will include:

Proof of death—either from funeral home or a death certificate;

Your Social Security number, as well as the worker's;

Your birth certificate;

Your marriage certificate, if you're a widow or widower of the deceased;

Your divorce papers, if you're applying as a surviving divorced spouse;

FINAL INSTRUCTIONS FORM

Name _____

Memorial Service
__ At home
__ At place of worship
__ At funeral home
__ Other_____

Disposition of Remains
__ Burial
__ Cremation
__ Embalming
__ No embalming
__ Open casket
__ Closed casket

Funeral Home Preference
Company:_____
Addresss:_____
Telephone: _____
Contact: _____

Cemetery Preference
Company: _____
Address: _____
Telephone: _____
Contact: _____

Documentation of Prepayment *(Please attach any paid receipts or contracts to this form)*
__ Memorial service
__ Funeral
__ Cemetery
__ Burial plot

Special Instructions

_____
_____
_____

Dependent children's Social Security numbers, if available;

Deceased worker's W-2 forms or federal self-employment tax return for the most recent year; and

The name of your bank and your account number, so that benefits can be directly deposited into your account.

If you are already getting Social Security benefits as a wife or husband on your spouse's record at the time of his or her death, you should report the death to Social Security, which will change your payments to survivor's benefits.

If you are getting benefits on your own record, you'll need to complete an application to get survivor's benefits. Call or visit your local Social Security office and an official will check to see if you can get more money as a widow or widower. To process your claim, Social Security needs to see an original or certified copy of your spouse's death certificate.

Benefits for any children will automatically be changed to survivor's benefits after the death is reported to Social Security.

How Much Will You Get?

The amount of your Social Security benefit is based on the earnings of the person who died. The more he or she paid into Social Security, the higher your benefits will be. The amount you will get is a percentage of the deceased's basic Social Security benefit. The percentage depends on your age and the type of benefit you are eligible for. Here are the most typical situations.

- Widow or widower, age 65 or older: 100 percent;
- Widow or widower age, 60–64: about 71–94 percent;
- Widow, any age, with a child under age 16: 75 percent;
- Children: 75 percent

There is a limit to the total amount of money that can be paid to you and other family members each month. The limit varies, but is typically equal to about 150 to 180 percent of the deceased's benefit rate. If the sum of the benefits payable to the family members is greater than this limit, the benefits will be reduced proportionately.

Veteran's Administration Benefits

If your loved one was already receiving monthly payments from the Veteran's Administration (VA), you will need to notify the VA of the death.

If the deceased was a veteran, he or she may be eligible for burial in one of the 115 national cemeteries, free of charge. Veteran's assistance may provide transportation of the remains to the nearest veterans' cemetery and a marker or headstone, as well as a flag. If you choose a veteran's burial, you will have to document the fact that the deceased was a veteran, including his or her separation papers (Form 214), and have proof of: rank and branch of the service, date of entry into and date of departure from the service, date of birth, date of death, Social Security number (his or hers as well as your own), and name and address of the executor or trustee of the estate.

If you use a private cemetery, you still can apply for a burial allowance, a flag, and a government headstone or marker from the Veteran's Administration. To apply, just look in the blue pages of your phone book for the number of the VA office nearest you, For more information, log on to *www.cem.va.gov.*

Employee Benefits

Many employers provide life, health, or accident insurance that may provide coverage you are eligible to make a claim against or to continue. The deceased may be due a final paycheck for vacation or sick leave. Be sure to contact all past employers, include federal, state, or local governments, to see if you are entitled to death benefits, continued health insurance coverage for the family, or payments from an annuity or pension plan. If the deceased belonged to a union or professional organization, check to see if it offers death benefits for members. Also find out about any credit union balances.

Funeral and Burial Costs

Funerals and burials are among the most expensive purchases older people make. The average cost of a traditional funeral is $4,600. A large part of this cost is for embalming, which you should know is not required by law unless you are transporting a body across state lines. Flowers, obituary notices, acknowledgment cards, burial liners or vaults, and special transportation can add an additional $1,000. In-ground burial costs another $2,400.

NEED TO KNOW
The Funeral Rule

The Funeral Rule requires funeral homes to provide price lists so that you know what options are available to you and exactly how much they will cost. Funeral homes, but not cemeteries, must disclose prices by telephone and offer price lists for review at each facility. Many funeral homes will mail you a price list, although the law does not require this. To obtain a copy of the Funeral Rule, call 877-FTC-HELP or log on to *www.ftc.gov/bcp/rulemaking/funeral*.

Most of us are unprepared to make wise financial decisions about a funeral and burial. We have little or no experience with making funeral arrangements. The emotions surrounding the death of a loved one—or contemplating our own mortality, if we are prearranging our own funeral—may cloud our judgment. It's never easy to make funeral and burial arrangements, but finding out about

them in advance is easier than coping with them at a time of need. If you want to know everything about the funeral industry, read Jessica Mitford's book, *The American Way of Death Revisited*. It is funny and very informative. In the meantime, here are some pointers:

• **Shop around for best prices.** Most of us select a funeral home or cemetery based on location, reputation, or personal experience. There is nothing wrong with that, but you may pay too much if you only call one facility. Call or visit at least two funeral homes and cemeteries to compare prices.

• **Compare prices for the entire package, not just a single item.** Every funeral home should have separate price lists for general services, caskets, and outer burial containers. Only by using all three lists can you accurately find the total costs and be able to compare prices. Be sure you buy only what you planned to buy. Try to keep in mind that the amount you spend on a funeral and burial is not a reflection of your feelings for the deceased.

Some of the services you are likely to be offered and/or charged for include:

• **Funeral director services** for initial conference, consultations, paperwork, and overhead. This fee is added to all bills.

• **Transportation of the body** to the funeral home and to the place of final disposition.

• **Care of the body,** including embalming and "casketing," or dressing the body.

• **Cremation**

• **Use of facilities** for a viewing, wake, or visitation, and the funeral or memorial ceremony at the funeral home.

• **Purchasing flowers**

• **Preparing obituary notices**

• **Providing music**

• **Immediate burial:** This is a simple, low-cost funeral. The body is interred without embalming, usually in a simple container. There is no viewing or ceremony with the body present. A package price for immediate burial will include the funeral director's fee, transportation, and care of the body. It may not include the charge for a container, casket, or simple pine box. Viewings are possible even if you choose not to be embalmed. The funeral home will refrigerate the body for a minimal or no fee. Be sure to ask about this option.

• **Direct cremation:** The package price for direct cremation includes the funeral director's fee, transportation of the body, and care of the body. It may not include the charge for cremation.

• **Casket:** Traditionally, caskets were sold only by funeral homes, but now cemeteries and third parties sell caskets, even on the Internet. Collect casket price lists from several funeral homes to compare prices of a particular model. Under the federal Funeral Rule, a funeral home cannot charge you extra if you provide your own casket from an outside source. No casket is required if you choose direct cremation, immediate burial, or to donate the body to science.

• **Grave liner or vault:** These outer burial containers surround the casket in the grave to prevent the ground from sinking, as settling occurs over time. In some locations, both funeral homes and cemeteries sell vaults and liners. In some areas, it is possible, and less expensive, to purchase an outer burial container from a third party. You can collect outer burial container price lists from several providers to compare the costs of a particular model.

• **Burial plot.** Even if you have already purchased a burial plot, you most likely will be charged an opening fee when the time comes to use the plot.

WHAT TO DO WHEN SOMEONE YOU LOVE DIES

_____ In the Estate Planning Documents folder in your Protection Portfolio, locate the final instructions form.

_____ If death took place in the hospital, you will be asked the name of the funeral home or cremation society of your choice, which will then make arrangements to transport the remains. Find out how much they will charge to transport the body.

_____ If death took place at your home or anywhere other than a hospital, then you have to contact the funeral home or cremation society of your choice, which will make the arrangement to transport the remains. Find out how much they will charge to transport the body.

_____ If you don't know which funeral home you want to use, ask your friends, your clergyman, or the local coroner.

_____ Ask a close friend of family member to help notify family and friends of death of your loved one.

_____ Make funeral, burial, or cremation arrangements. Be clear about embalming, as it is expensive and not required by law.

_____ Order at least 15 certified copies of the death certificate. You will need them in order to collect insurance proceeds and to change name on bank accounts, deeds, and other assets.

_____ Try not to leave the house vacant, as this may have consequences for insurance coverage. Ask a friend or family member to stay at the home, or at least have them check in on a daily basis to water plants, collect mail, and care for pets.

_____ If you do not already have one, open a bank account in your own name.

_____ If you do not have a credit card in your own name, request one. After you have received your own card and credit limit, advise the credit card company of your loved one's death.

_____ Before paying any credit card debts that were not yours, check with your attorney or executor. If there isn't enough money in the estate to pay off the debts, the probate has a "schedule" specifying debts given priority and the order in which the debts are to be paid — which is why I want you to check with your attorney before you begin paying the debts.

_____ Go to your Protection Portfolio and remove your loved one's insurance policy. In addition to life insurance, check to see if other forms of insurance covered the deceased. Some loans, mortgages, and credit card accounts are covered by credit life insurance, which pays off account balances. Contact each insurance company about how to claim the policy benefits.

_____ Contact your local Social Security, Veterans Administration, deceased's employer's human resource office, or visit their Website to see if there are any benefits that you qualify for.

_____ Your own will or trust should be changed now, for most likely you left everything to the person who has just died. Make sure you change the beneficiary designation on your IRA, life insurance policies, pension plans, 401(k) plans, and other investment or retirement plans.

FUNERAL HOME COST WORKSHEET

	Funeral Home #1 _____ Phone #_____ Contact _____	**Funeral Home #2** _____ Phone #_____ Contact _____	**Funeral Home #3** _____ Phone #_____ Contact _____
Funeral director fee			
Transportation of the body			
Care of the body			
Cremation			
Use of facility			
Flowers			
Preparing obituary notices			
Providing music			
Immediate burial			
Direct cremation			
Casket			
Grave liner or vault			
Burial plot			
Total			

Tax Records

Chapter Eleven

TAX RECORDS

Please locate and store the documents listed in the "Tax Documents Checklist" at the right and file each document in your Protection Portfolio. If you have a complicated tax return, you may find that the Protection Portfolio does not have adequate space to house your complete tax return. If this is the case, please make photocopies of only the tax return forms that you submitted to the IRS for each of the last three tax years and place those copies in your Protection Portfolio. Store complete tax returns, along with all supporting documentation, in another secure location.

Please note: If you do place your tax returns in a location other than the Protection Portfolio, attach a note to the Portfolio tax file explaining where the complete returns are stored, both as a reminder to yourself and as a convenience to family members.

Taxes and the Road to Wealth

Whenever I ask people, "What's the one thing you have the hardest time with when it comes to your money?" a surprising number answer, "Taxes." As inevitable as death, as inevitable as springtime, taxes are inevitable for all of us; although we may fret over them and postpone them, in the end we must compute them and pay them.

Why are we so obsessed with taxes? It's not as if we can control them. Over the years, most of the tax write-offs we used to read about or take advantage of have been disappearing, one by one. Whether you are rich or poor, there is now very little you can do to manipulate your tax bill. Of course, you can invest with tax consequences in mind, but minimizing taxes is rarely the main concern of sophisticated investors; making money is. In fact, people who are in control of their money, people who have power over their money, and people who are certain of their goals for their money are least likely to worry about taxes. Whether you are rich or poor, you will worry more about your taxes if you feel less powerful over your money.

Why is that? Because, in the end, the amount you pay in taxes is simply one measure of the amount of wealth you are creating for yourself and your loved ones. With that in mind, figuring out

---

TAX DOCUMENTS CHECKLIST

Last three years of tax returns, plus supporting documentation of income and expenses, including:
- ❏ W-2 forms
- ❏ 1099 forms
- ❏ Documentation of home improvement records
- ❏ Documentation of medical expenses
- ❏ Documentation of donations to charities
- ❏ Documentation of investment expenses
- ❏ Investment income records, such as records of interest and dividends received
- ❏ Capital gains records, including records of the sale of homes, stocks, bonds, or other capital investments
- ❏ Documentation of employee business-travel and entertainment expenses
- ❏ Documentation of higher-education expenses
- ❏ Documentation of student loan interest payments
- ❏ Documentation of real estate taxes, mortgage interest, closing costs

---

your taxes to the best of your ability—including getting the help of a tax accountant, if you need it—and paying them with a grateful heart is the way to go. If you end up paying more in taxes than the next person, it means that you've earned more and will also get to keep more. And that's one more step forward on the road to wealth.

How Long to Keep Your Tax Returns

How long you need to keep your tax returns will depend on the type of return you file. For a more complete list of tax documentation and how long to keep it, please refer to "Documents to Keep" on page 11 of this guidebook. In general:

• *If your taxes are relatively simple, keep documentation for three years,* which is how long the IRS has to audit you once you've filed. Keep your return, W-2 forms, 1099 forms, records of investment income and other income (rental income, for example), and records of tax deductions.

• *If your returns are more complicated, keep documentation for seven years.* If you claim capital gains or losses, if you have your own business or are self-employed, if you have inherited considerable sums of money, or if you have bought or sold a lot of property and if the IRS thinks you have not reported all your income, it can audit you as far back as six years. To be on the safe side, keep seven years' worth of returns and documentation.

If the IRS suspects you of big-time cheating, it can audit you for any year it chooses. If, God forbid, you have actually committed fraud, your papers won't do you much good, but you probably ought to keep them.

What You Need to Know about the Economic Growth and Tax Relief Reconciliation Act of 2001

In my opinion, the most important thing to understand about the 2001 tax reform bill is the underlying message it is intended to send to all of you. That message is: Be careful.

With this bill, the government is implicitly saying to all middle-class Americans, "You do not have enough money saved for your retirement, and we know that. Therefore, beginning in the year 2002, we are going to allow you to save more money in tax-advantaged retirement programs, such as IRAs and 401(k)s. But there's a good chance that we'll only let you do this for a limited number of years—that is, until this bill begins to cost the government too much money in lost tax revenues and we repeal it." For built into this bill is an automatic repeal date: the year 2011.

As you read over the list of text reductions on the following pages, I want to emphasize as strongly as I possibly can that each and every one of these tax-savings benefits is set to expire in 2011—and any or all of could be repealed at any time before then. So please, please, please learn about them now and act on them immediately. Please protect your future by acting now to bolster your retirement savings and reduce your tax bill. The opportunity may not come gain.

How to Protect Yourself Against an Audit

I have never implied that the IRS is not a powerful agency. If you make a serious mistake in calculating or documenting your taxes—or even if the IRS just thinks you did—it can audit you. Nobody in his right mind wants to go through the worry, effort, and expense that an audit can entail. But it can be avoided—by taking most or all of the nine steps listed here:

1. Report all income for which you have received a tax statement (W-2, 1099-MISC, 1099-DIV, 1099-INT), and make sure that there are no discrepancies between tax statements and your return.
2. Attach all required forms and supporting schedules to your return.
3. File on time.
4. Have a competent tax professional prepare or review your tax return.
5. Adjust your exemptions to avoid receiving large refunds.
6. Before applying for a home-office deduction, make sure you qualify. Don't exaggerate working space or make aggressive home-repair deductions.
7. Avoid taking a deduction for donations that are out of line with the income you've reported. If you donate more than $500 of goods (not cash) to charities, fill out Form 8283.
8. Don't round off to the nearest $50 or $100.
9. Be neat and legible.

Major Tax Law Changes by Year
2002

• **Income tax.** Each of the top four federal rates drops. (See chart.) New 10-percent rate takes effect.

• **529 College Saving Plans.** Withdrawals are tax-free.

• **Educational Savings Account.** Top annual contribution rises to $2,000. Tax-free withdrawals can be used for qualified K-12 expenses as well as college expenses. Income eligibility rises for married couples to $220,000.

• **Higher education deduction.** Deduct up to $3,000 a year in higher education expenses (if you earn less than $65,000, for single filers, or $130,000 for joint filers. The deduction is phased out if your AGI exceeds $80,000 for single filers and $160,000 for joint filers).

• **Student loan interest loan deduction.** Deduct up to $2,500 a year in interest payments on your student loans, no matter how long you've been paying them.

• **Estate taxes.** Estate and generation-skipping transfer (GST) tax exemption rises to $1 million. Top federal estate tax rate drops to 50 percent. State death-tax credit is reduced from its 2001 levels by 25 percent.

• **Traditional and Roth IRAs.** Top annual contribution rises to $3,000. For those age 50+, top contribution rises to $3,500.

• **401(k)/403(b) and government 457 plans.** Top annual contribution rises to $11,000. For those age 50+, the top annual contribution rises to $12,000.

• **SIMPLE.** Top annual contribution rises to $7,000. For those age 50+, top contribution rises to $7,500.

• **SEP-IRA.** The dollar cap and the maximum percentage of income you can contribute have gone up. You can contribute up to a $40,000 cap or up to 25 percent of your compensation, whichever is less.

• **Adoption.** One-time credit rises to $10,000.

2003

• **Estate taxes.** Top federal estate tax rate drops to 49 percent. State death-tax credit is reduced from its 2001 levels by 50 percent.

• **401(k)/403(b) and government 457 plans.** Top annual contribution rises to $12,000. For those age 50+, top contribution rises to $14,000.

• **SIMPLE.** Top annual contribution rises to $8,000. For those age 50+, top contribution rises to $9,000.

2004

• **Income tax.** Top four rates drop. (See chart.)

• **Higher education deduction.** Deduct up to $4,000 a year in higher education expenses (if you earn less than $65,000 for single filers, or $130,000 for joint filers. The deduction is phases out if your AGI exceeds $80,000 single filers and $160,000 married, joint filers).

• **Estate taxes.** Estate and GST Tax exemption rises to $1.5 million. Top federal estate tax rate drops to 48 percent. State death-tax credit is reduced from its 2001 levels by 75 percent.

• **401(k)/403(b) and government 457 plans.** Top annual contribution rises to $13,000. For those age 50+, top contribution rises to $16,000.

• **SIMPLE.** Top annual contribution rises to $9,000. For those age 50+, top contribution rises to $10,500.

2005

• **Married standard deduction.** Rises to a level that is 174 percent of the deduction for single taxpayers.

• **Child credit.** Rises to $700.

• **Estate taxes.** Top federal estate tax rate

How Income Tax Rates Decrease 2002-2006

The top four tax rates will fall as follows. (Tax rates during the period 2002–2006.)

Tax Year beginning	28%	31%	36%	39.6%
2001	27.5%	30.5%	35.5%	39.1%
2002 or 2003	27%	30%	35%	38.6%
2004 or 2005	26%	29%	34%	37.6%
2006 or later	25%	28%	33%	35%

drops to 47 percent. State death-tax credit is repealed.

• **Traditional and Roth IRAs.** Top annual contribution rises to $4,000. For those age 50+, top contribution rises to $4,500.

• **401(k)/403(b) and government 457 plans.** Top annual contribution rises to $14,000. For those age 50+, top contribution rises to $18,000.

• **SIMPLE.** Top annual contribution rises to $10,000. For those age 50+, top contribution rises to $12,000.

2006

• **Income tax.** Top four rates drop again. (See chart.)

• **Married standard deduction.** Rises to a level that is 184 percent of the deduction for single taxpayers.

• **Estate taxes.** Estate and GST tax exemption levels rise to $2 million. Top federal tax rate drops to 46 percent.

• **Traditional and Roth IRAs.** For those age 50+, top annual contribution rises to $5,000.

• **401(k) and similar plans.** Top annual contribution rises to $15,000. For those age 50+, top contribution rises to $20,000.

• **SIMPLE.** For those age 50+, top annual contribution rises to $12,500.

2007

• **Married standard deduction.** Rises to a level that is 187 percent of the deduction for single taxpayers.

• **Estate taxes.** Top federal tax rate drops to 45 percent.

2008

• **Married standard deduction.** Rises to a level that is 190 percent of the deduction for single taxpayers.

• **Estate taxes.** Estate and GST tax exemption levels rise to $2 million.

• **Traditional and Roth IRAs.** Top annual contribution rises to $5,000. For those age 50+, top contribution rises to $6,000.

2009

• **Married standard deduction.** Rises to a level that is 200 percent of, or twice that of, single taxpayers.

• **Child credit.** Rises to $800.

• **Estate taxes.** Estate and GST tax exemption levels rise to $3.5 million.

2010

• **Child credit.** Rises to $1,000.

• **Estate taxes.** Federal estate tax is repealed.

2011

• **The sunset provision.** Unless the U.S. Congress extends the Economic Growth and Tax Relief Reconciliation Act of 2001, every single provision of the new law, as itemized above, will disappear and the old rates and limits will return, just as they stood in 2001.

FINAL WORDS

I hope that you and your family will benefit all your lives from using the Protection Portfolio System.

When it comes to money, there's a universal rule that I believe applies to everyone. It tells us that we must be careful of our thoughts, because our thoughts become our words. We must choose our words carefully, because our words become our actions. And we must remain conscious of our actions, because our actions become our habits, and our habits become our destiny.

Nowhere is this truer than when we are planning for the care and protection of our loved ones in the event of our incapacity or death. If we let procrastination and other forms of fear keep us from making a plan and sharing it with those who most need to understand it, our destiny and the destinies of those we love can be altered dramatically, and permanently, for the worse.

That's why I created the Protection Portfolio System. I wanted to make it easier for you to bring your best thinking and your actions into alignment to insure the safest possible future for you and your family. I hope that you have used all the relevant elements of the Protection Portfolio System to put into place all the forms and documents that you and your loved ones will need. I especially hope that each and every one of you now has—or is in the process of getting—a will, a revocable living trust with an incapacity clause, a financial durable power of attorney, and an advanced directive and durable power of attorney for health care.

It's my deep and true belief that once you have these things in place, the love you think you have and the love you say you have for those closest to you will grow and blossom into the richest kind of security and happiness. That is what I wish for you.

With all my love and respect,

ABOUT SUZE ORMAN

Suze Orman has been called "a force in the world of personal finance" and a "one-woman financial advice powerhouse" by *USA Today*. She is the author of four consecutive *New York Times* bestsellers: *The Laws of Money, The Lessons of Life; The Road to Wealth; The Courage to Be Rich;* and *The 9 Steps to Financial Freedom;* and the national bestsellers, *Suze Orman's Financial Guidebook* and *You've Earned It, Don't Lose It.*

Suze's latest book, *The Laws of Money, The Lessons of Life* (The Free Press; March 2003), was launched with a cross-country bus tour that took the author to 21 cities as part of her groundbreaking grassroots campaign to help people across America gain control of their money. Instantly hitting the *New York Times* list, it also appeared on the bestseller lists of *Publishers Weekly, The Wall Street Journal, USA Today,* the *Chicago Tribune, The Boston Globe,* and the *Los Angeles Times.* The book already has 600,000 copies in print.

The Road to Wealth (Riverhead Books) became a *New York Times* bestseller after just one week on sale and currently has more than 650,000 copies in print. Among the top 15 nonfiction bestsellers on *Publishers Weekly*'s 2001 hardcover list, the book also placed in the top ten on both *USA Today* and *Business Week*'s business bestseller lists for 2001. The book appeared simultaneously on *The Wall Street Journal*'s hardcover nonfiction and business bestseller lists, and held positions on the bestseller lists of the *Los Angeles Times,* the *San Francisco Chronicle, The Washington Post,* and the *Chicago Tribune,* as well.

An instant number-one *New York Times* bestseller, *The Courage to Be Rich* (Riverhead Books) currently has more than one million copies in print and was among the top ten nonfiction bestsellers on *Publishers Weekly*'s 1999 hardcover list. The book was also number one on the business bestseller lists of *USA Today* and *The Wall Street Journal,* where it appeared simultaneously on the *Journal*'s hardcover nonfiction bestseller list. In addition, it made *Business Week*'s bestseller list, reached the number-one position on the *Los Angeles Times* list, and held spots on the bestseller lists of *The Washington Post,* the *San Francisco Chronicle,* the *Chicago Tribune,* and *The Boston Globe.* The trade paperback edition of *The Courage to Be Rich* has close to 300,000 copies in print.

Suze's other number-one *New York Times* bestseller, *The 9 Steps to Financial Freedom* (Crown Publishers) has 2.1 million copies in print in its hardcover edition. Remaining on that list for more than 11 months, the book was the number-one nonfiction bestseller on *Publishers Weekly*'s 1998 hardcover list. It also held the top spot on the bestseller lists of many publications nationwide, including *The Wall Street Journal, USA Today, The Washington Post,* the *San Francisco Chronicle,* and the *Chicago Tribune.* It is currently available in six countries worldwide.

Among *USA Today*'s top ten business bestsellers for 2001, the trade paperback version of *The 9 Steps to Financial Freedom* (Three Rivers Press) has close to 800,000 copies in print, with a total of ten printings. Immediately hitting the *New York Times* bestseller list, the book ranked third on *Business Week's* list of paperback business bestsellers for 2001, and appeared on the bestseller list of *The Wall Street Journal*, as well. Running Press published a miniature hardcover edition of the book in 2001. *Suze Orman's Financial Guidebook*, a quick reference resource for putting the *9 Steps* to work, has more than 180,000 copies in print after five printings.

Suze Orman's first book, *You've Earned It, Don't Lose It* (Newmarket Press), which was originally published in 1995, is currently in its 28th printing with more than 700,000 copies in print in its combined hardcover, softcover, and audio formats. It appeared on the bestseller lists of *Business Week*, *The Wall Street Journal*, and *USA Today*.

Suze has written, co-produced, and hosted four PBS specials based on her bestselling books. The most recent, which was inspired by *The Laws of Money, The Lessons of Life*, premiered nationwide in March 2003, and instantly joined the previous three as among the most successful fundraisers in the history of Public Television.

Profiled in *Worth* magazine's 100th issue (October 2001) as among those "who have revolutionized the way American thinks about money," Suze was a 2003 inductee into the Books for a Better Life Award Hall of Fame in recognition of her ongoing contributions to self-improvement. Previously, Suze had received the 1999 BBL Motivational Book Award for *The Courage to Be Rich*. As a tribute to her ongoing involvement, in 2002, the organization established The Suze Orman First Book Award to honor a first-time author of a self-improvement book in any category. She recently received a 2003 Crossing Borders Award from the Feminist Press. The award honors a distinguished group of women who not only have excelled in remarkable careers, but have also shown great courage, vision, and conviction by forging new places for women in their respective fields. In 2002, Suze was selected as one of five distinguished recipients of the prestigious TJFR Group News Luminaries Award, which honors lifetime achievement in business journalism.

The personal finance editor on CNBC, Suze hosts her own national CNBC-TV show, which airs every weekend. She recently garnered an American Women in Radio and Television (AWRT) Gracie Allen Award for *The Suze Orman Show* in the National/Network/Syndication Talk Show category. The Gracie Allen Awards are given to those who strive to encourage the positive and realistic portrayal of women in radio and on TV.

Suze is a contributing editor to *O: The Oprah Magazine*. She appears regularly on QVC as host of her own "Financial Freedom" hour. Among her phenomenally successful proprietary product launches on QVC was the nine-volume *Ask Suze Financial Library*, which sold 400,000 sets. Additionally, she has joined forces with GE Financial, a wholly owned subsidiary of GE Capital, to offer *Suze's Choice*, a GE Long Term Care Insurance plan tailored to deliver the benefits she believes are essential when considering the purchase of this type of insurance.

Suze Orman, a Certified Professional Planner® professional, directed the Suze Orman Financial Group from 1987–1997, served as Vice President of Investments for Prudential Bache Securities from 1983–87, and from 1980–83, was an Account Executive at Merrill Lynch. Prior to that, she worked as a waitress at the Buttercup Bakery in Berkeley, California, from 1973–80.

A sought-after speaker, Suze Orman has lectured widely throughout the United States and South Africa, helping people change the way they think about money. She has been featured in such major publications as *Newsweek, People, The New Yorker, Modern Maturity, The New Republic, USA Today, The New York Times*, and the *Chicago Tribune*. She has also appeared on *Dateline*, CNN, MSNBC, *Good Morning America, The View*, and numerous times on *Larry King Live* and *The Oprah Winfrey Show*.

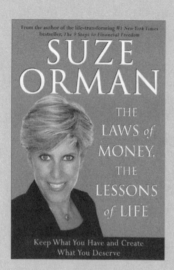
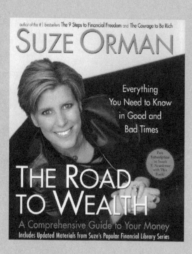

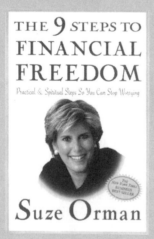
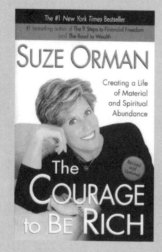

NOTES

NOTES

NOTES

NOTES

NOTES

NOTES

Emergency Contacts

Executor of The Will / Trustee
Name_____
Phone #_____
Accountant
Name_____
Phone #_____
Attorney
Name_____
Phone #_____
Family Doctor
Name_____
Phone #_____
Friend/Family Member
Name_____
Phone #_____
Friend/Family Member
Name_____
Phone #_____

Emergency Contacts

Executor of The Will / Trustee
Name_____
Phone #_____
Accountant
Name_____
Phone #_____
Attorney
Name_____
Phone #_____
Family Doctor
Name_____
Phone #_____
Friend/Family Member
Name_____
Phone #_____
Friend/Family Member
Name_____
Phone #_____

Emergency Contacts

Executor of The Will / Trustee
Name_____
Phone #_____
Accountant
Name_____
Phone #_____
Attorney
Name_____
Phone #_____
Family Doctor
Name_____
Phone #_____
Friend/Family Member
Name_____
Phone #_____
Friend/Family Member
Name_____
Phone #_____

SUZE ORMAN'S PROTECTION PORTFOLIO
SUZE ORMAN'S PROTECTION PORTFOLIO
SUZE ORMAN'S PROTECTION PORTFOLIO

Emergency Contacts

Executor of The Will / Trustee
Name_____
Phone #_____
Accountant
Name_____
Phone #_____
Attorney
Name_____
Phone #_____
Family Doctor
Name_____
Phone #_____
Friend/Family Member
Name_____
Phone #_____
Friend/Family Member
Name_____
Phone #_____

Emergency Contacts

Executor of The Will / Trustee
Name_____
Phone #_____
Accountant
Name_____
Phone #_____
Attorney
Name_____
Phone #_____
Family Doctor
Name_____
Phone #_____
Friend/Family Member
Name_____
Phone #_____
Friend/Family Member
Name_____
Phone #_____

Emergency Contacts

Executor of The Will / Trustee
Name_____
Phone #_____
Accountant
Name_____
Phone #_____
Attorney
Name_____
Phone #_____
Family Doctor
Name_____
Phone #_____
Friend/Family Member
Name_____
Phone #_____
Friend/Family Member
Name_____
Phone #_____

SUZE ORMAN'S PROTECTION PORTFOLIO
SUZE ORMAN'S PROTECTION PORTFOLIO
SUZE ORMAN'S PROTECTION PORTFOLIO

Emergency Contacts

Executor of The Will / Trustee
Name_____
Phone #_____
Accountant
Name_____
Phone #_____
Attorney
Name_____
Phone #_____
Family Doctor
Name_____
Phone #_____
Friend/Family Member
Name_____
Phone #_____
Friend/Family Member
Name_____
Phone #_____

Emergency Contacts

Executor of The Will / Trustee
Name_____
Phone #_____
Accountant
Name_____
Phone #_____
Attorney
Name_____
Phone #_____
Family Doctor
Name_____
Phone #_____
Friend/Family Member
Name_____
Phone #_____
Friend/Family Member
Name_____
Phone #_____

Emergency Contacts

Executor of The Will / Trustee
Name_____
Phone #_____
Accountant
Name_____
Phone #_____
Attorney
Name_____
Phone #_____
Family Doctor
Name_____
Phone #_____
Friend/Family Member
Name_____
Phone #_____
Friend/Family Member
Name_____
Phone #_____

SUZE ORMAN'S PROTECTION PORTFOLIO
SUZE ORMAN'S PROTECTION PORTFOLIO
SUZE ORMAN'S PROTECTION PORTFOLIO